A Prophet
and a Scribe

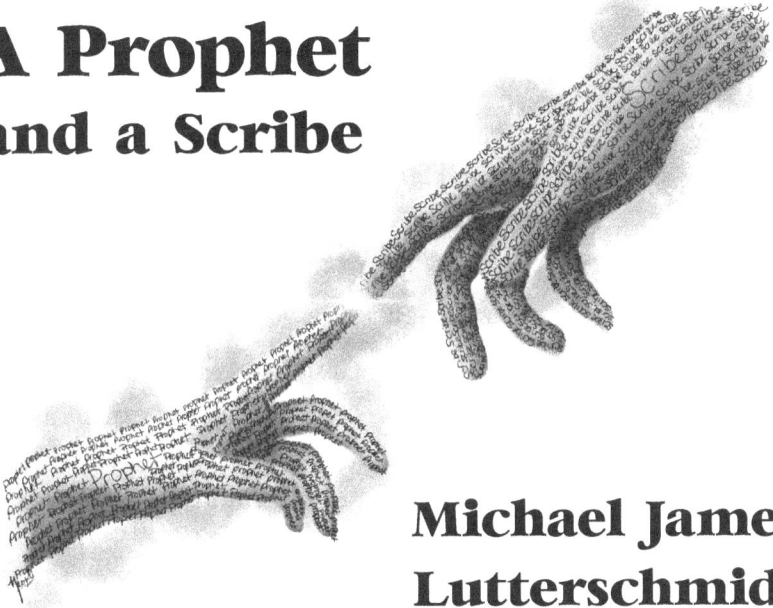

Michael James
Lutterschmidt

Wisdom
Editions
Minneapolis

Wisdom Editions

SECOND EDITION DECEMBER 2022

Cover and interior design by Gary Lindberg
Cover and interior illustrations by Neordi

ISBN: 978-1-959770-81-7

A Prophet
and a Scribe

Contents

Dedication

Daniel and I would like to thank everyone who participated in this project. A special thanks to Nelson Diaz (Neordi) for helping us visualize some of our stories with his artwork. As always, without the love and support of my mother and father, Lou and Agnes Lutterschmidt, this journey would have never been realized.

I want to thank Gary and my publishing team. Gary's role in my last three projects has been more that a mentor than a publisher. His expertise and wisdom helped bring together each book and his partnership went far beyond editing and publishing.

I also want to dedicate this journey to my daughter, Lila Lutterschmidt. Honey it has been about six years since I have been able to hug you. Throughout these last few years and the last three books, I have left a trail of breadcrumbs for you to discover the war I have been fighting for you every minute of the day. Pure evil and horrific lies of sorcery and deceit took us away from each other. When the time comes, I know that you will be strong enough to accept the truth. You are my blood and you are very special. Although I may be gone to speak these words to you in person, trust you are destined for very special things in this life. Always listen to your heart.

Finally, to people who are suffering in this world... to the Targeted Individuals who are getting tortured and slaughtered... to the innocent pawns being used by federal criminals to engineer mass murder—trust, I will use every beat of my heart and my very last breath to prevent the Illuminati from enslaving every man, woman and child.

As it is written, it must be so.

Also by the Author

Extrajudicial Execution: The Dying Testimony of
Michael James Lutterschmidt

Rambling of a So-Called Paranoid Schizophrenic

Introduction

The world is full of mystery, magic, and power. People possess different levels of awareness of these hidden and perhaps forbidden truths. People achieve an awakening through different means. While individuals are born with varying gifts, others find a way to educate themselves through experience, education and detoxification. Very few , however, are born with the ability to connect with the powers of the universe and possess the dedication to comprehend their true potential.

Consider the accomplishments of the most influential people throughout history and you will discover they have tapped into both natural and learned powers. As a human race, we learned to fly because of the combined power of will and the understanding of the universe. I want you, the reader, to understand how certain powers exist that the average person will never acknowledge. Some of these enchanting powers include astral projection, time travel, human flight, telekinesis and even the ability to speak and communicate with spirits of the past and future.

Nostradamus was one of the most well-known prognosticators of all time. His awareness and ability to predict future events is legend. But perhaps he wasn't psychic at all. Maybe he was born with the ability and fortitude to access information from the future. Perhaps he learned how to tap into the abilities of time travel to see these future events with his own eyes. If you lived in the 1400s, how would you describe large flying objects? I would probably describe them as steel birds. Interestingly, Nostradamus's magic may be a truth hidden in plain sight.

What if Nostradamus actually saw two "steel birds" destroying two immense towers six hundred years before it happened? Would that ability to see such a future event stop those horrific acts from happening? What good comes from such a power if we don't find a purpose for it?

I am currently being crucified. I have written two books while being tortured and poisoned by thousands of ignorant people. So, what is my purpose? What good can come from my crucifixion? So far, the combination of my pain and willingness to accept that pain has guided me to putting my story and knowledge on paper. I have communicated truth to my daughter for her future acknowledgment. I have exposed a multitude of heinous acts of evil committed by those once related to me. My documented education and personal suffering regarding mold and mycotoxins may help countless others find help and relief. I have written words which may have exposed child trafficking, forcing legal action against the most powerful empire in the world. My words have led to a federal grand jury to review evidence of revolutionary acts of espionage. My awareness and newfound perceptions have created a magical empowerment along with a deadly responsibility.

I write for therapy. This emotional release has essentially led me to document the communications I receive no matter what their origin. Professionals term this release as automatic writing that helps me ignore the psychological warfare while making a stand for humanity. I believe there are minds in our world that are fighting to expose certain secrets. Suffering cruel inhumanity as a targeted individual, I am eager for the Great Awakening.

My purpose is not to persuade you to believe me. I have been gifted an awareness about certain things, and my purpose is to document that awareness. Please understand that my acceptance and willingness to endure this induced pain is my demonstration of faith. No matter how much I am abused, tormented, slandered, poisoned and destroyed, I blindly accept my purpose.

A person's higher power communicates through various shapes and forms. This form of communication may come from events, situations and predicaments you deal with every day. It is only your awareness that allows you to hear, see and understand these communications. The people around you may be influenced by your higher power to provide answers and guidance. These may occur through random encounters or friends and family who enter your life with purpose.

An evil force can enter your life in the same fashion. Evil provides a more blatant form of communication that causes you to ignore subtle cues of good. Free will gives us all the power to choose who or what we listen to and how we proceed to act. Please understand our humanity is currently under attack. A dark, Luciferian force is using covert weapons of mass destruction to exterminate our God-given free will.

To this day, I am uncertain why a man named Daniel Collazo came into my life. Despite all the evil that surrounds me, Daniel has been and continues to be a true friend, a brother. I have learned he possesses a magical awareness many people cannot comprehend. Among his gifts is telekinesis, developed through education and detoxification. He can rebuke demons and was born with other spiritual or supernatural gifts. Perhaps this is the reason Daniel has become a brother. I am constantly surrounded by evil, and maybe Daniel's ability to overcome evil will help me in my war against Lucifer.

I may be in his life for a reason as well. Based on my ability to document my own reality, perhaps Daniel's higher power is working through me to help him find his true potential, his own purpose in this life. And so I will begin capturing the life of Daniel and documenting some of his stories, which will illustrate his enchanting gifts, abilities and beliefs. Since we are beginning with no true end in mind, I will be working through the experiences of this project, which will hopefully lead us to a purpose. I have faithfully embraced my role as the scribe of a prophet.

An Early Voice

Daniel was born on May 3, 1981. He grew up in Dunkirk, New York where he lived with his mom and stepdad. Daniel was also close with his biological father early on, but separation of a child's biological parents can impact the child. Daniel moved around a lot while growing up. Not only were his parents separated, everywhere he moved he was always the new kid. It must have been difficult forming relationships with people only to move away and start anew.

From probing into Daniel's past, I have learned he was not only burdened with a destructive kind of modern-day upbringing, but he has been a focal point of an unimaginable spiritual battle for Daniel's soul. Even at a young age, evil forces have been trying to diminish his will. Sometimes, as you may know, the people in your life may be used as a tool in such a battle. For whatever reason, a dark force is terrified of Daniel's true potential. Daniel has confessed to me many acts of evil perpetrated against him. I believe that dark force has been trying to hinder and even destroy the power of his spirit.

Daniel grew up as a Christian Pentecostal. He frequently attended Bible studies but often found himself alone during his adolescent years. He didn't have any stable relationships and only a few role models. One of these role models was Brother Jake, a religious, guitar-playing supporter who communicated with Daniel obliquely and subtly in a way the unempowered could not have understood.

Brother Jake had suffered trauma himself. He had a nasty scar on the back of his neck, which provided instant attention and unwanted feelings from those he interacted with every day. The disfigurement wasn't important to Daniel. It was the way Brother Jake behaved despite the unwanted sympathy that impressed Daniel who usually described his friend as inspirational, loving, and genuinely happy, as if God had said to Daniel, "Do you see the real man?"

Daniel thought, *how could someone with such a scar be so happy and loving*? The insights Daniel had gave him the power to understand the persuasive evil around him, which I believe is still trying to hold him down. *If Brother Jake can find peace and happiness, then why can't I*? Daniel concluded.

I don't want to focus on my life here, but I believe I have been gifted with a responsibility to share my perceptions. I have a scientific brain that correlates with my PhD siblings. I just don't have a degree on the wall to prove my knowledge. Whenever I formulate a perception, I know better than to make it absolute. There will always be future persuasions which lead to deeper truth. With that said, I see the possibility I may be involved with Daniel more than I had originally thought.

Daniel knew he was special from the beginning. This type of conviction can only be experienced by those who are gifted enough to acknowledge that the feeling exists. As a young boy, Daniel explained to me, he heard noises in his closet followed by the clattering footsteps of a small creature. As he hid under the covers, he felt this small creature crawl onto the bed and scamper up to his chest. Suddenly, two fighting cats began screaming and the creature scurried off, disappearing into the darkness of the closet.

After several nights of being tormented this way, Daniel had an awakening. No one told him how to approach this situation. But one night courage came over Daniel and he projected his power. He confronted the dark shadows of his closet and shouted, "By the power of Jesus, you have no power here! You're not welcome! Be gone!" Perhaps his Bible studies gave him the notion to speak out in Jesus's name, rebuking the creature of darkness. Sister Karen was another influence on Daniel's faith. She directed him to seek answers in the Bible, so he did.

The creature-in-the-closet event reminded me of the movie *Cat's Eye,* in which a small troll appeared from behind a wall to drain a little girl of her breath. If it wasn't for a heroic cat, the demon may have succeeded.

Daniel believed that he was awake and aware during his encounter with a small demonic creature in his bedroom. He believed he had full access to all five senses—and most likely a sixth. If you dive into the lore and do the research on demon-like trolls, you will find mind-boggling evidence dating back to the beginning of time. Daniel's encounter makes me want to learn more.

Daniel's beliefs and experiences led him to become a thrill seeker. I will describe his successful boxing career later, but Daniel told me he learned how to fight in his dreams. Of course, watching Bruce Lee movies before he went to sleep may have influenced his dreams.

Driven to test his own invincibility, Daniel decided to pull off a stunt he was convinced he could accomplish. On a playground swing, he swung to the highest point and then attempted a back flip to the ground. As Daniel came off the swing wrong, he found himself heading headfirst toward a collision with the hard dirt below. He closed his eyes and clenched every muscle in his body awaiting the inevitable crash with the unforgiving turf.

The way he described the event to me was as if someone had caught him and gently laid him to the ground. Time and gravity no longer existed to Daniel during this fall. Lying on his back, he opened his eyes after what he described as a prolonged descent to earth, much longer than the 1.03 seconds it should have taken. Nonetheless, Daniel finally opened his eyes as he safely lay on his back looking up at the pendulum swing.

If Daniel had only described this encounter himself, I would not have the well-formed perception I hold today. However, Daniel's close, non-relation aunt witnessed this event and explained it as if something had grabbed Daniel in midair and gently placed him on the ground. She stated, "That boy is special."

Earlier I mentioned that communication from good forces is much more subtle than those of evil forces that are used to dampen the human spirit. Daniel began seeing shadows, hearing noises, and sensing various types of paranormal activity pretty much every place he traveled. Then, one night, a higher power spoke words to Daniel at the influential age of thirteen.

Daniel stumbled out of bed and walked into the bathroom. He sat on the toilet with his head in his hands, still dozing lightly. Suddenly, he heard his name spoken. It wasn't enough to bring him back to full consciousnesses, but the voice gave him enough of a jolt to come out of whatever state of sleep he was in. Daniel looked around and began to understand he was only dreaming. Then, while awake in the dark, the voice called his name again. He stood up to look out the window. No matter how much he concentrated, he could not tell if someone else might be present. He sat back down and thought about going back to bed. Then, like a bolt of energy, "Daniel!" was shouted with great ferocity and he felt the presence of a being in front of him.

The voice was like an electronic shock sending vibrating impulses throughout his body. Daniel was desperate for answers. If I were to guess, 90 percent of the population in Daniel's age bracket would have crawled back into bed and pulled the covers over their heads. Over time, the experience would diminish to coincidental meaninglessness and this obvious communication would be forgotten.

Daniel spent the next few hours looking around outside. He checked every room in the house, every closet, and even some of the large cabinets. A voice he both heard and felt did not come from someone hiding in the house or outside the window. This was a *spiritual* awakening. He began to seek answers and even question his own purpose.

To some, coincidences are random and meaningless events. To a few empowered individuals, however, they are an acknowledgement of something purposeful and meaningful. The similarity, frequency, and patterns of coincidences can help clarify their meaning.

Daniel's name had been mysteriously called out three times, with each utterance more powerful than the last, leading to a surge of electrocution-type vibrations throughout his body. I can say with certainty that he believes this voice was not from this world.

If you pay attention, random patterns and experiences often provide a message. Only a few seek to acknowledge and understand these messages. Was there a scientific explanation to explain the voice Daniel heard? Psychiatry, psychology, sociology, acoustics, probability and every other field of study could provide a distinctive hypothesis. So, I began to search for other patterns and frequencies related to random voice-to-skull phenomena.

Being a targeted individual (TI), I am more alert to these types of phenomena than most. I know my TI family gets tortured with all kinds of new age, science fiction weapons. One of these experiments includes the "God Voice," also known as "Voice to Skull" or "V2K." This technology allows sadistic people to transmit voices into a person's head using radio frequencies and sound waves. Usually, these abusers say horrible things to the victim and the goal is to collect data. Based on the frequency and patterns of V2K I have uncovered, I do not believe this to be the case for Daniel. So, allow me to suggest a non-technology possibility. What is the opposite of technology? I believe it to be spirituality and faith.

I don't believe you can get any more opposite of technology than the Bible, one of the most influential books of humankind. In the Bible, the Lord calls Samuel when Samuel is just a boy studying under Eli. Samuel lies down in bed and hears a voice call his name. Samuel replies, "Here I am," as he runs to Eli.

Eli responds by telling Samuel he did not hear a voice and tells him to go back to bed. As the boy lies down, trying to get comfortable, he closes his eyes only to again hear his name called out even more powerfully than the last time.

A second time, Samuel called back, "Here I am" and ran into Eli's sleeping quarters. Again, Eli replies, "go back and lie down." This happens a third time and finally Eli understands a higher power is communicating to Samuel. This time, when Eli tells Samuel to go back to bed, he also instructs Samuel to respond with acceptance.

The Samuel story provides a message of compliance to God's will, but I cannot exclude the similarities to Daniel's story. In the Bible Samuel's word spreads to Israel. Is it possible that a power exists that can widely spread Daniel's message to the masses?

My goal as a scribe is to discover the purpose of Daniel's calling. What message are we supposed to spread?

Daniel didn't have a mentor to tell him to respond with awareness and acceptance. Daniel was left to his own conclusions. Perhaps if someone would have guided Daniel, he might have received more clarity from his experience. Daniel relied on his human instinct to seek a rational explanation.

Based on my perceptions, I conclude Daniel heard a "God Voice." I believe that scores of other people also get some form of this power every day. Unfortunately, many contributing factors push these random coincidences off their memory maps.

Daniel grew up and moved around Pennsylvania a few times. He was able to reconnect with his father in Johnstown, Pennsylvania and they later settled in the Lehigh Valley. Daniel and I chuckle sometimes about becoming brothers and residing in Bethlehem.

Due to the way he grew up, Daniel focused on what he thought was interesting, which took time away from his schoolwork. In many areas of study, though, Daniel is knowledgeable. He studied message therapy and natural healing. He also studied and dedicated time to working with the mentally challenged.

Perhaps to release aggression, he began studying Tai Chi and boxing. With every experience and unexplained coincidence, Daniel learned more. He began to acknowledge and accept the various forms of communication sent to him and developed an understanding of the paranormal. My own inability to fully understand some of Daniel's encounters creates a passion to seek more understanding.

The Shadow Entity

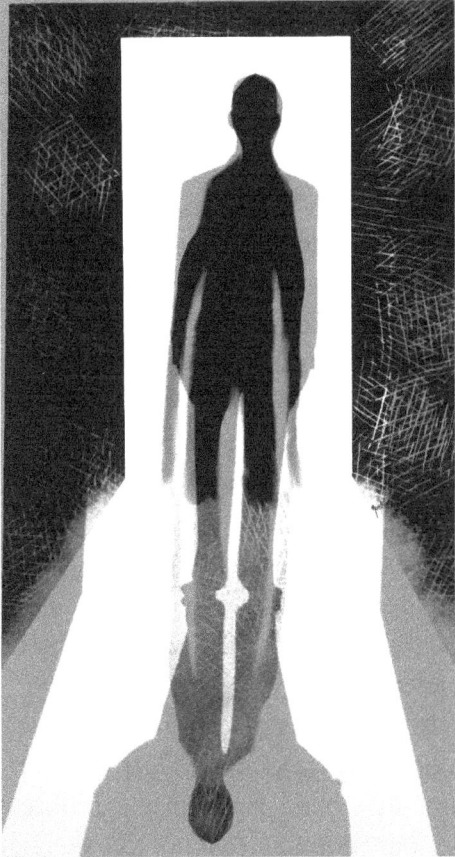

For whatever reason, at an early age Daniel possessed a sixth sense about situations and people. For example, one day at a family gathering he pointed at two of his female cousins and warned that demons were following both of them—a peculiar thing to say in adolescence. Daniel's aunt, who had overheard Daniel's bold statement, explained, "Trouble has followed those girls their entire lives."

As the scribe, I encourage you to pay attention to the consistency and frequency of these experiences. While many people overlook patterns and allow these events to fade away over time, I am listening intently, trying to understand the meaning of these events.

After a few sessions with Daniel, I am documenting some examples to support my belief that a war of good versus evil is underway. Daniel's stories provide clues. Whatever evil surrounds Daniel is fearful of his power. I am still unclear as to what this power may be. The sessions that make up this book are my process for developing a better understanding. Currently, Daniel and I are fumbling through our method. With each session, our minds are connecting on a magical, even spiritual level.

Daniel eventually joined his father in Johnstown by moving in with a friend, Pedro. As soon as Daniel walked into his new house, he felt the presence of a paranormal energy. For whatever reason, Daniel was still suppressing these forms of communications, so he ignored his ability to sense this other world.

During a time of intimacy with a girlfriend, they both felt a heavy, ominous entity in the room. She confirmed with Daniel her own awareness of this presence, and they both admitted hearing accompanying noises. Daniel could feel this power, and whatever it was, it didn't make itself visible—yet. He could feel temperature deviations and the tickle of body hair standing up on end, suggesting electromagnetic energy.

Daniel's sixth sense was always in overdrive even though he often chose to ignore the awareness. During this instance, though, he didn't *see* anything. And he didn't feel threatened by these paranormal communications, at least not like the fear he'd felt when the troll climbed up onto his chest. Perhaps this dark force was using the people around him to indirectly attack Daniel. Having discovered earlier that he could rebuke a demon, Daniel knew he was in no real danger. The people around Daniel were not as fortunate.

My focus in this session will be on the evidence and testimonies from eyewitness accounts. To accurately document these stories, I want to consider as many explanations as possible. My personal perceptions, which I am starting to solidify, will hopefully guide me to some form of reasoning or purpose.

The people around Daniel did not have the same warding power that he possessed. These people sometimes came into terrifying contact with a powerful entity that never identified itself physically to Daniel. I ask myself, *Why* not? Was this entity trying to get to Daniel by terrorizing those around him? Was there a reason why this figure never made physical contact with Daniel?

One night, after arriving home, Pedro was walking to their front porch. As he was putting the key into the front door, the door suddenly opened, and he was greeted by a large, dark shadow. Pedro described a dark, seven-foot-tall figure. There was little light, but Pedro recalled an evil expression on the figure's face. Then the entity turned into the house and moved into the kitchen. Pedro was terrified! Common sense intruded as he searched for a logical explanation. He called out to his roommate Daniel, who was not home.

Pedro followed the figure into the kitchen, desperate to find some reasonable explanation. He turned on the kitchen lights, but no one was there. He then checked the bathroom, bedrooms, and the living room. Clearly, whoever or whatever had opened the door to greet him was no longer in the house.

Pedro nervously fled the house and rushed down to a local bar to wait for Daniel to get out of work. Pedro tried to explain the details of his encounter. Daniel, however, was unsure about the meaning behind the message delivered by the entity. Maybe Daniel chose to block out the obvious signs so he could feel somewhat normal. Nevertheless, they both went home and tried to move on from this experience.

Following that incident, while Pedro was walking home from the laundromat one night, he had another encounter. Across the street was a parking lot. The lot was blocked off by a chain connected to a vertical pole. Pedro saw the same entity that had opened the door now sitting on top of the pole and staring right back at him with a sinister smirk.

It would be nearly impossible for a seven-foot-tall man to sit eerily calm while balancing on a pole designed simply to support a small chain.

Chills shot down Pedro's spine as the eyes of this dark figure followed his every stride. Pedro looked straight ahead and hurried his pace home. When he saw his doorstep up ahead, he grabbed his keys from his pocket and glanced back to this figure. He was gone. Pedro stopped and looked all around, though he was alone on that street. He walked in and again told Daniel about his encounter with this entity.

Daniel felt something instantly when he moved into that house. He knew there was an unbalance, but what was he supposed to do about it? Daniel had to work and pay bills like everyone else. It's not like he went to school to learn how to stop dark shadow figures from terrorizing people. When Daniel learned of the second encounter, he couldn't help but to think Pedro was being used as a gateway.

Pedro's fear, I believe, allowed the energy of the entity to grow stronger. He constantly heard peculiar sounds. The more fear Pedro exhibited, the more interaction the shadowy entity created.

A few nights later, Pedro awoke from sleep gasping for air. He'd been startled awake by a tremendous pressure on his chest, and he tried to get his eyes to focus in the dark of the room. Wheezing and terrified, Pedro suddenly saw the now-familiar seven-foot entity standing on his chest and looking down with that familiar, creepy grimace. Pedro tried to scream, but no words would come out. He prayed for help and finally Pedro was able to call out, "Daniel!" The figure immediately looked at the door then stepped off his chest and vanished into the darkness.

As I analyze these reported events, I obviously consider Pedro lying on an average-size bed with a seven-foot-tall figure standing on top of him without bumping the ceiling. The picture I form in my mind doesn't make sense to me. But I remember Daniel mentioning that Pedro slept on a mattress on the floor. This cleared up the height issue, though Pedro sleeping on the floor suggested something else to consider.

We sleep above the ground for obvious reasons. Many species sleep in the trees to avoid predators lurking below. Perhaps Pedro sleeping on the floor gave an open invitation to an already charged-up energy. Maybe we have learned to sleep above the ground not just to protect us from creatures of this world, but those not of this world as well.

From that night forward, Pedro slept on a reclining chair in Daniel's room. Pedro truly felt safer when he was around his roommate, for obvious reasons. Whatever this entity was, it seemed to avoid Daniel. When Pedro called out for his roommate by name, this dark presence vanished.

Before long, the stress and fear from these events began to break down the will of Pedro. He eventually moved out of that house and wished Daniel good luck.

Over the next few weeks, Daniel learned that a mother and her children had moved into an apartment directly above. He would often greet a babysitter who came and went frequently. Although Daniel didn't have the chance to get to know the new neighbors well, he sensed the family was in danger.

One day, as the babysitter was leaving, Daniel asked the young woman if it would be OK to ask a personal question. The woman answered, "Sure, what's up?"

"Do you guys ever hear or see strange things in your apartment?" Daniel asked.

The babysitter's face turned white and she looked befuddled. She told Daniel that he should ask the mother because she didn't want to overstep parental choices about certain strange occurrences. She told Daniel, however, that the mother was working just down the street and inferred that the "situation" had become quite dire.

Daniel walked down the street and greeted the mother at her job. She recognized him from the building but didn't know his name. He introduced himself as the neighbor downstairs and said, "Would you mind if I ask you something personal about you and your family?"

Confused, the mother nodded. Daniel asked if she felt safe in the apartment. A sense of relief flushed over the mother's face. I know that when something is causing you grief and cannot be easily explained or understood by others, it can be refreshing to find another person who might understand.

The mother poured out the experiences she and her children had been having. They would often hear noises, footsteps and voices. Items would get mysteriously moved around and the overall energy in the apartment seemed "dark." Her son, who was about five years old, was receiving the brunt of the torment. The boy would wake up in the middle of the night, jump out of bed and race down to his mom's room screaming. He would complain that there was a tall, dark man is in his room.

The mother confided her feeling of total helplessness. She said she was going to have someone come over and bless the house since she didn't know what else to do. Daniel only alluded to Pedro's experiences because he didn't want to add to the fear, which is what these evil entities feed on. Fear is what makes them grow stronger.

Daniel knew that calling someone to bless the house could cause more harm than good. He doesn't fully understand how he knows such things—he wasn't accredited with a fancy degree and he didn't spend years away studying—but he possessed certain innate knowledge. Every unexplained event that has occurred to him has added to his awareness.

Daniel knew that if the person who tried to bless the house did not believe, the energy of the entity would grow stronger. A good analogy is the "poker face." When you have a terrible hand but still want to play, you have to bluff by putting on a poker face. Some of these entities have special powers that allow them to know if there is a real threat, or if the enemy is just an impostor. Also, if a person doesn't understand exactly what he or she is trying to get rid of, the method used will be just a guess and possibly wrong. The force Daniel and his neighbors were dealing with had enough power to make itself known physically. They couldn't afford to guess at the remedy.

Nevertheless, the mother scheduled a priest to bless the house and hoped for the best.

A few weeks passed before Daniel again encountered the mother outside. He asked her how everything was going and saw fear in her watery, bloodshot eyes.

She asked Daniel if he has seen or heard anything. He said, "Sometimes I hear you guys in the middle of the night. But no, that entity doesn't come around me." He asked if the blessing had helped at all. She replied that for about a week the apartment was quiet. Everyone was sleeping well, and the family had started to believe it was all over. "And then just the other night," she said, "things got so much worse."

The woman looked downward, defeated and scared.

I personally believe this week of peace was the result of their own actions, not the priest's blessing. By coming together as a family unit and hoping for the same outcome created energy, they had temporarily kept that dark entity at bay. After the first stress-free night, the family developed a positive belief which boosted their power to fight the entity.

I believe in laws of attraction where positive thoughts will bring positive outcomes, and vice versa. A great power exists within group meditation. As I continue to document these stories, I am beginning to see glimpses of the joint purpose of Daniel and I, and it is amplified by the powers of meditation.

The combined positive family thoughts, however, grew shallower over a short period of time. The family was beginning to get back to normal and tried to forget the events. It is possible that their efforts to forget allowed the entity to sneak back into their lives. Perhaps it was one bad emotion—or one sin—that broke down the wall.

It isn't easy to pick up and move a family. You need a security deposit and two months' rent in advance to be considered for another apartment, plus gaining a black mark on your record for breaking a lease. Daniel saw this family's desperation and decided to act. He wasn't trained or well-studied, but he had innate knowledge about useful things. He knew something had to be done to save this family. Looking straight into the woman's eyes, Daniel said with complete confidence, "Don't worry, I got this."

How could Daniel even know where to begin? What made him believe he could help this family, and who gave him the notion of where to start? Instead of fretting, though, he just acted.

Daniel went home and burned incense to smudge his apartment. He made sure to enter every space to spread a positive energy. In the living room, Daniel fell to his knees and began to meditate. He committed to himself that he had the power to rebuke this dark entity and help the family. Belief itself is a powerful magic, and it has been documented in the scriptures how faith alone can move mountains.

Daniel put his head to the ground and asked the Lord to help him protect the woman and children upstairs. "Please send the most holy and worthy angels of the highest power to see over me," he prayed.

Daniel suddenly felt a warm wave of power and he knew that all he had to do was "will" this demon away. He sat in silence and focused all his energy on removing the entity from the house forever. The power of his thoughts, much like the family's group thoughts, was the answer to banishing this dark shadow. After that night of intense meditation, the family never experienced another episode.

So, if I am on the right path, consider how the group thought and family belief was strong enough to get rid of this shadowy demon for a week. Then consider the power that Daniel possesses. His personal meditation and prayer was enough to banish the demon for good. What amazes me is that Daniel never had a teacher. He doesn't have years of specialized education, which means the power he is tapping into is just the tip of the iceberg. What could Daniel do with the right direction and understanding? Maybe part of my role in this journey is to help him discover these gifts.

Could this be the answer for our own humanity? The concepts of group meditation and communal prayer has been practiced for centuries.

We are experiencing a great deal of evil in our world today. Currently, we are under quarantine for a worldwide Covid-19 pandemic. I believe this virus defines the very evil of which I speak. I am not the only person who believes this pandemic was planned and intentional. This pandemic is an engineered bacterium activated by 5G technology. There are very few who understand the intentions of the perpetrators, though. Stephen Covey wrote in *Seven Habits of*

Highly Effective People, "Begin with the end in mind." So, what is their "end in mind?"

Perhaps if we came together as a human race and prayed for the same positive outcome, our combined energy would banish Lucifer back to hell. It is said that a Tulpa is an energy created from the power of group thought or belief. Some claim many cryptids today are the result of a group of people believing in those creatures, so powerful is group thought that it can bring these things to life. The legends of the Jersey Devil or the Thin Man are good examples. It may be possible that group belief and focused prayer could create the power we need to survive an apocalyptic holocaust.

Much like Daniel, I believe we all possess a certain level of magic. Perhaps my purpose is to begin an awakening through my writing. We all have a power. If we bring our powers together for a common good, humanity can accomplish anything. This is God's gift to us. He does not work for us. Our Holy Father works through us.

Daniel knows he has unique abilities. He just doesn't know why. Like every man, he must work and provide. Life gets in the way of our desire to search for our own true purpose. In my previous book, *Ramblings of a So-Called Paranoid Schizophrenic*, I defined this concept as social conditioning. Even though life gets in the way, the journeys we have begun, combined with our own beliefs, kindle a yearning.

I need to learn more about the life of Daniel and how his life connects with my own. I am hungry for more communication.

Session III

The Power of Will

As I learn more about the life of Daniel, many of my original thoughts and perceptions are becoming more lucid. I am enchanted by the consistency and frequency of the paranormal events Daniel has experienced throughout his life. It seems that everywhere he goes and everyone he meets is somehow burdened with a form of a communicative presence that is not of this world. Even Daniel's own son has become a focal point of this energy.

While still in a relationship with his son's mother, they all once lived together in a house that coincidentally was also haunted. As I mentioned earlier, everywhere Daniel goes, there are powers waiting for him.

In the haunted house, Daniel and his family heard screeching noises, doors slamming shut, footsteps, voices and many other disturbances. Perhaps it is Daniel himself who is haunted, or he is simply a magnet for such phenomena. Despite attempts to discover logical explanations for the hauntings, Daniel found none.

On one occasion, Daniel heard something fall in his son's room. When he walked in, he saw one of his son's battery-powered cars lying tipped over on the floor. The wheels were still turning. Cindy, the grandmother of Daniel's son, went to turn off the car, but to her amazement the wheels kept turning for a while. When she tried to remove the batteries, she discovered there were none installed.

Paranormal research has been studying these types of interactions with our world for a very long time. Devices have been created to pick up electromagnetic energy that is said to be the fingerprints of such paranormal entities. Spirit boxes are used to allow an easy means of communication between the physical and spiritual worlds using radio signals. Ouija boards have been used for centuries to communicate with spirits. Many investigators claim spirits and entities use electronics to demonstrate their presence because it is an easier means to cross the veil.

My goal is not to prove paranormal phenomena exists or try and convince you Casper the friendly ghost is real. My intent is to discover a purpose as to why Daniel is confronted with so much supernatural activity—not just the occasional noise or ghostly encounter, but aggressive, sometimes even violent interactions.

Here is another example. One night, Daniel's infant son woke up screaming. Daniel sleepily went to check on his son, but the baby wasn't in his room. Daniel suddenly realized the screams were coming from the downstairs kitchen. How could this have happened? Daniel's son was in a playpen behind a locked door. How could a one-year-old baby get out of the playpen, open a locked door, get over the baby gate at the top of the stairs and make it downstairs onto the kitchen floor?

I hope you are beginning to understand there are forces in our world which we cannot possibly understand. The amount of energy required to move a child like this is unimaginable, which is why so many brainwashed, ignorant skeptics refuse to believe such a thing could happen.

During our session together, Daniel skipped around on his own personal timeline. He spoke about a woman named Stephanie. Stephanie became a partner for Daniel and their relationship proved so serious that they dedicated eight years to each other. One day, while Daniel was working, Stephanie went to check out a place for them to live. The house worked well logistically, though a strange feeling came over Stephanie when she entered the building. She had trouble explaining her feelings, but she felt a presence around her. For whatever reason, she chose to ignore her experience and didn't mention it to Daniel at the time.

As soon as Daniel walked into this new place, he got chills and instantly felt a wave of energy. He looked at Stephanie and asked if she had felt that sensation.

Stephanie replied, "Oh my God, I didn't want to say anything, but yeah—I felt something the first time I saw this place."

Daniel replied, with no doubt in his tone, "This place is haunted."

As I said earlier, many people receive some form of otherworldly communication but choose to ignore it. Sometimes, though, this energy is so charged that you cannot ignore the communication.

Wherever and whoever Daniel meets is forced to confront a powerful entity. Look at my own life. I started this project with the hope of finding more purpose for Daniel since we have become brothers. Currently, I am fighting a war against a Luciferian force. I direct you to my previous books for more information. Perhaps Daniel will be able to help me win this war and banish Lucifer, this time for good.

Some people may share one or even a few paranormal events. Entire shows and movies have been created about such real-life encounters. For whatever reason, Daniel was a magnet for this kind of activity. He didn't just seem to attract this energy—he was able to *control* this power as well. Perhaps this is why no entities ever threatened Daniel directly but rather terrified the people around him.

Session III with Daniel became intense when I learned about Stephanie's sister, Sandy, who lived nearby. I learned that Sandy was another gateway who had been introduced into Daniel's life, and she was being terrorized by something. One day, while Stephanie and Sandy were talking in another room, Daniel overheard Sandy complain about some frightening events in her house.

In addition to the usual haunting phenomena such as noises and sounds, Sandy's children showed signs of being physically attacked. At first, these phenomena were overlooked, but once scratches and bruises appeared, the reality became too obvious to ignore.

Then Sandy pulled out a video shot during the previous holiday. She had footage of her Christmas tree levitating in midair. The power of the energy must have been strong enough to make physical, violent contact with the children and sufficient to lift a full-size tree into the air.

Because Daniel had just moved into a house with Stephanie which had such energy itself, he interrupted their conversation and pulled Sandy away from Stephanie. He expressed his concern for Stephanie's mental well-being and said he wanted to lessen her growing fears. Daniel knew that fear allows certain entities to grow stronger. If Stephanie began to fear her own home, whatever energy was in the house could be strengthened.

As soon as Daniel finished speaking, they heard a knock on the basement door. The pets were not in the room, the kids were not around, and there was no logical explanation for the knocking.

Daniel told Sandy to keep that little event to themselves so Stephanie's anxiety would not increase. They left the room and found Stephanie in the living room taking pictures, as if trying to capture proof of something after seeing the video of the tree floating in air and the scratches on the children. She was photographing everything.

At last, she and Daniel reviewed the pictures she had taken, curious to see if she had captured anything paranormal. They were astonished to see a glowing orb in the room with them. As Stephanie was scrolling through the pictures, the orb grew larger and closer, frightening Stephanie. Daniel tried to calm her down and convince her it was just dust particles catching the light, but he knew the truth. Once again, as soon as Daniel finished his statement, a picture hanging over the fireplace flew off the wall as if someone had thrown it toward them.

These two events in a short period of time —the rapping on the basement door and then the orb and soaring picture—were clearly a response to Daniel. Both events had occurred after Daniel had spoken calming words attempting to belittle or discredit the entity's power. Whatever this was, it did not want to be ignored.

So far, I have learned that Daniel has the ability to rebuke some of these entities. The little troll-like creature vanished when he willed it gone. The shadowy figure that terrorized Pedro and the family living above had disappeared after Daniel meditated, prayed, and spread his will throughout the house. He possesses a magical awareness and seems to relate to the supernatural. In addition, certain powers may be looking out for his well-being.

Why does Daniel experience these frequent encounters, and more importantly, for what reason? Why does Daniel get these communications but most people don't?

Stephanie was at home with Daniel one day talking with Sandy on the phone. Sandy was explaining to Stephanie that she had been diagnosed with a cancerous brain tumor. This was tragic news, of course, and Stephanie was devastated by it.

Shortly after confiding in Daniel about her sister's tragic diagnosis, something came over Daniel. He described the event as losing control of his own body. Feeling as if a higher power had taken control of his mind, Daniel told Stephanie, "Take me to your sister. I will make the tumor go away."

As Daniel described this experience to me, his non-verbal cues directly matched his surrendering emotions. Using all forms of communication, I believe Daniel was confused by these events and even a little scared. His eyes were tearful.

Daniel sincerely does not understand what made him say those words to Stephanie or how he knew he could help Sandy. He just knew it. Eventually, they went to see Sandy and she was in good spirits considering the situation. Although Sandy seemed to be doing fine, the tumor was malignant and growing.

After that visit, Daniel prayed. Like the time he rebuked the shadowy figure, he just acted. Daniel was never taught this skill. He didn't have anyone telling him he could do this type of magic. He just knew. In my eyes, his action defines faith. My own action to blindingly document his experiences defines my own faith. We both seem to be listening to a communication, merging our efforts into a combined belief. We will find a purpose.

Daniel meditated and prayed in silence for Sandy. He imagined the tumor shrinking away and disappearing. He begged the heavenly father to give Sandy a second chance. Daniel didn't directly communicate this prayer to Sandy. Stephanie overheard his prayer but wasn't fully accepting of what Daniel claimed he could do.

At Sandy's follow-up appointment, the doctors were flabbergasted. Somehow, the tumor decreased in size. Maybe there was a scientific explanation. Perhaps the tumor's shrinkage was coincidental nonsense. I believe otherwise, which is the entire reason for documenting these events. In addition to his other gifts, I now believe a suppressed ability to heal has been awakened in Daniel.

So, for what purpose? Is there a greater intent, a larger meaning? I need to seek more understanding. I need to explore a personally consuming, emotional connection. With each thought and every event I capture, the more vivid I see Daniel's memories. I can honestly say there were times I became lost in my head, or perhaps in Daniel's, drifting off into what seemed like a daydream while listening to Daniel share his encounters.

Because I'm afraid I'm not painting the picture well enough, I will use a movie to help me clarify. Ebenezer Scrooge paints my picture perfectly. The concept of Scrooge watching the reenactments from his life—past, present and future—are exactly how I have begun to witness Daniel's memories. I find myself hovering above Daniel, as if I had traveled back in time—into *his* time—and somehow can see, hear, and feel what he is experiencing.

I am not sure what to label this phenomenon, and I could easily let it fade from memory. I am not making claim to any special abilities. I must take my own advice and acknowledge how these increasingly vivid sessions could be a unique form of communication between Daniel and me.

Laws of Attraction

Daniel and Stephanie were together for almost a decade. The emotional equity involved with a long-term relationship sometimes cannot compete with life changes. I have always described relationships as pieces in a jigsaw puzzle. First you stumble through those adolescent years and learn about the opposite sex. During this period, you are picking up pieces of a puzzle to see which one fits. This is where you start to gather the edges of your picture. Then you start looking for the interior pieces by shape, color and size. Over time you get better at looking for the pieces you need before even picking them up. In a relationship, if you try to use the wrong piece, it doesn't quite fit and it will eventually skew the entire picture.

The challenges of life arise because life changes people along the journey, which in turn changes relationships. Throughout life you have to put together a few different jigsaw puzzles. As a scribe's piece of advice: Don't keep the wrong piece jammed in for too long. Keep looking, eventually you will find the piece you are looking for, which will help you put together the bigger picture.

Daniel's abilities were not limited to the supernatural. He possessed a strong intuition about people as well. Perhaps this is why we connect so well.

Daniel began to sense a change in Stephanie's overall personality. Maybe her perception of her current jigsaw picture started to pour out through nonverbal communications. Just as Daniel could sense otherworldly entities, he could sense Stephanie slipping away from the person he once knew. Daniel starting catching her in lies, but for whatever reason he continued to believe her deceits.

When you love someone, but your own personal jigsaw puzzle changed, it is terribly hard to say goodbye to the *old* picture because of the emotional equity involved. Many people hold onto the old picture while trying to figure out what the new puzzle looks like. This is where communication, understanding and compassion needs to prevent anger and evil to overcome our emotions. I want to stress my belief in this because it is anger and evil that provides energy to demonic entities all around us. Not only did Stephanie hide from these feelings, but she used drugs and alcohol as a means of escaping the emotional stress of this life change. This form of escape never helps the situation, but instead invites negative energy into your life. Allow me to prove my point while I document this next session with Daniel.

During this period in Daniel and Stephanie's relationship, an uncomfortable change in the overall jigsaw picture went unacknowledged and therefore buried its energy into their emotions. I will claim, based on my understanding and beliefs around laws of attraction, that this negative energy created a fuel for entities around them. Remember, Daniel is already a magnet for these events.

One night while Daniel was working at the local Pizza Bar and Restaurant, he received a call from Stephanie about a local power outage. She felt uncomfortable and a little frightened being home alone in the dark. Daniel tried to calm her down, assuring her that the power would soon be back on. Daniel went about his night at work, but a little while later he got a terrifying call from Stephanie. She claimed something was chasing her in the house, but due to the power outage she couldn't see anything. Daniel said, "Relax, don't feed into it," as he had often counseled in the past.

As she was lying in bed under the covers behind a locked door, she frantically tried to explain to Daniel what she had just seen. As she'd been walking around the dark house, she said she could feel something following her. This "energy" appeared to be inseparable from the shadows. Standing in the entrance to the living room, she stared at the other side of the room where the fireplace was located. As her eyes tried to adjust to the darkness, a stationary, shadowy figure started eerily moving away from the fireplace toward her.

Stephanie cried into the phone, "I was standing there looking at this shadow, and then I saw it come right at me, like it was charging me!" Stephanie ran into the bedroom, locked the door and jumped under the covers to call Daniel, pure terror in her voice.

Daniel calmed Stephanie down, reminding her that whatever it was, it had no power over her. He assured Stephanie, "Everything will be fine," and within minutes the power was restored. Coincidence?

Some time passed and Stephanie was no longer able to hide her new jigsaw puzzle. Life dredged up her past and it began to flow into her current life. Daniel knew she was sneaking off to see an ex-boyfriend from many moons ago, and her denials created a great deal of negative energy.

As a scribe, allow me to provide a message to all the readers. No matter what jigsaw puzzle you have in your life, you cannot forget about the pictures of the past. Sometimes those puzzles were never completed before starting a new one. That hole where a piece is missing leaves an emptiness inside. When that old picture presents itself to you again, sometimes the shared emotional equity reignites a passion. This is human nature, which is why I spoke earlier about the importance of communication, compassion and understanding. Without these skills, we are just animals.

Toward the end of their relationship, the arguments between Daniel and Stephanie became violent. The physical abuse Daniel endured from scratches and slaps was no comparison to the verbal attacks. Stephanie loved Daniel, but she had become very confused about her own purpose. She escaped from this confusion and lack of direction through the use of drugs and alcohol. Daniel began to realize he too deserved the right jigsaw piece for his own puzzle.

After the separation from Stephanie, Daniel moved across the state to reconnect with his father in my home town of Allentown, Pennsylvania, which brought Daniel across my path. A few years would still come to pass before Daniel and I would work together and discover our spiritual brotherhood.

It was 2010 and I was at the highest peak of my life. I was making incredible money, I had success and fame, a beautiful wife and a daughter. I believed I was invincible. Toward the end of that year, however, my life began to fall apart on a biblical scale. While Daniel was making a life-changing decision, Lucifer was systematically destroying my life.

For the next year or so, Daniel went to school for massage therapy. He had always been interested in the connection between the body and mind. He wanted to free people from pain and stress. In addition to studying the school curriculum, Daniel passionately sought knowledge on his own. He began to experiment with cleansing, going days and even weeks with just water. He learned through his own discipline how a person can achieve enlightenment through a healing process known as fasting. The detoxification allows the mind and body to communicate more effectively. In 2011, Daniel committed to a forty-day fast. For that entire time, he consumed only water.

As Daniel was purifying his body by allowing his mind to become more awake, I was experiencing a complete toxic shock. My body and mind were being digested by mycotoxins and endotoxins from a mold-infested home purchased out of greed. To make matters worse, I was using amphetamines to try and counter the extreme fatigue. Much like Stephanie's situation, this coping mechanism invited a terrifying, dark energy into my life.

I believe Daniel and I share a similar purpose. In 2011, Daniel was beginning his path to a spiritual awakening while I began an awakening of my own. I do not believe this was a coincidence. We both felt an unexplained need to act.

A few years of preparation were ahead for both of us. While Daniel lived with his dad, he worked a few different jobs and attended school. One job was at the casino. Coincidentally, I also worked for the casino. We didn't know each other at the time, but I wonder if this was our higher power trying to work out the details for our paths to collide.

Daniel was used to always being the new kid and had developed a sincere desire to help other people. He rode public transportation to and from school every day. A girl named Geysha rode the same bus.

One day Daniel overheard Geysha telling another passenger how she wanted to listen to music on her phone but didn't have the earphones to do it. AI technology has brainwashed the youth of today, so I will mention the cell phones of that day were just getting started with these convenient capabilities.

The next day, Daniel brought in a pair of headphones that would work on her phone. This stranger on the bus was grateful and Geysha's first impression of Daniel was that he was a typical guy who naturally wanted something in return. Of course, Daniel didn't look at Geysha that way—he was just trying to help her out. It took a while for Geysha to acknowledge Daniel's sincerity.

After that, Geysha and Daniel began to talk more frequently, and a friendship formed. One day, Daniel overheard Geysha say, "I wish I could download my music." At the time, this capability wasn't like the live streaming of today. Daniel had a device that could make Geysha's wish come true. The next day, Daniel brought her the device, and the friendship grew even stronger. Knowing Daniel very well today, I know he would have done this for anyone.

Geysha invited Daniel to come to her house after school. After they downloaded the music, Daniel and Geysha went out on the balcony of the apartment building. They began to talk as friends, and as a sign of acceptance, Geysha invited Daniel to attend church with her. This began a conversation about God and their religious beliefs.

Daniel commented, "I love my Holy Father so much that if he told me to jump off a bridge I would do it, only because I know he will never ask me to do that." After a few minutes of them both getting absorbed in an enlightened conversation, they both heard a demonic growl come from the bottom of the stairs. This growl was a deep, thunderous vibration that could both be felt and heard. Geysha was startled and confused. Her mind searched for an explanation. Daniel looked at Geysha with a desensitized, conditioned empathy.

Daniel has been experiencing these odd paranormal events his entire life. This phenomenon had become commonplace in his life.

Geysha asked Daniel, "what was that?"

Daniel replied with a question of his own. "You mean the demonic growl?" Then, without emotion, he said, "That was a demon."

Geysha didn't know how to respond, so Daniel said, "I am going to try and continue our conversation, but you are going to start to remove yourself." Daniel knew that the dark force surrounding him did not like him inspiring other people. He knew from previous experiences how this paranormal disruption would inhibit their religious conversation. And that is exactly what happened. Geysha began to change the topic and eventually moved back inside. It had become evident that whatever power, ability, or knowledge Daniel tried to project onto others had displeased the demonic forces that surround him.

Daniel had become almost desensitized to these odd occurrences and I believe this gave their friendship more of a building block. Soon, they began to study together. Geysha would help Daniel with their assigned classwork and in return Daniel taught Geysha about fasting, religion and different theories of natural healing.

One day, they made plans to study for the night. She was going to stay over at Daniel's house so they could catch the bus together the next day. Geysha and Daniel walked to her house first so she could get her overnight bag. As they were walking back to his apartment, the sun was still out—not a typical time to see a paranormal event.

As they walked closer to a wooded patch near the apartment building, Geysha thought she saw a few "humanlike" figures scatter through the opening of the woods and then disappear into the thick shrubbery. Geysha didn't want to seem crazy, but after she had heard the demonic growl with Daniel, perhaps she felt a little more comfortable about questioning such things.

Geysha timidly asked Daniel, "Did you see that?"

For some reason, Daniel often responds with another question. He looked at Geysha with genuine sincerity and said, "You mean the shadow figures that ran off into the woods?"

It was hard for Geysha to grasp the reality of this situation. Not only did she see something, but Daniel seemed familiar with whatever she had seen.

Geysha looked at Daniel and said, "You have to do something."

"Yes, I know," he said. Daniel knew he possessed some type of awareness, but did not fully understanding why he was constantly surrounded by these events. And it was exhausting.

At this time, Daniel was also detoxifying by fasting. It has been noted how one of the early symptoms of this type of cleansing is a false ego. Fasting not only cleanses the body, but also the mind and spirit.

The way Daniel responded to Geysha's request for him to do something was egotistical. He said he knew, then shrugged it off, much like the rest of the world. He just didn't want to be bothered at the time.

As a brother to this man today, I want to share my own opinions to support the magnitude of this burden. Imagine that everywhere you travel you see a clown that no one else can see. The clown blows his obnoxious horn, but you are the only one who hears the intrusion. When you visit a friend, the clown is there. When you take a walk, the clown is with you. Imagine the solitude that comes from not being able to talk about this clown because no one else can confirm that the clown exists. This could be maddening.

Trust me, as a Targeted Individual not being able to get others to understand what I endure is enough to break your mind, which is the Illuminati's strategy in our current war. I am dealing with many people, no matter how wrong or evil they may be. Daniel is dealing with something entirely different. Once again, I must document how our lives have come together so perhaps I can find a reason for it all.

Daniel doesn't just have to deal with one clown. He deals with multiple paranormal entities that provide constant communication through all five senses. Whether it is some dark entity that is physically harming people to something mysteriously catching him in midair, Daniel is constantly surrounded by strange phenomena. The weight of this knowledge and the events Daniel experiences are difficult for the average person to understand. This isolation creates a hardened attitude.

The lack of attention Daniel gave to Geysha about the scurrying shadow entities pushed this episode out of their minds, and it was soon forgotten. Daniel later started to pray. He wanted to know why Geysha was experiencing these events when she was with Daniel. He wondered if Geysha was in trouble or needed help.

Perhaps his prayers created a memory map of Geysha needing help or advice. Maybe his focused energy created an ability to see outside of his own reality. That night, while Daniel was sleeping, he had a dream about Geysha getting into an argument with her mom. Because the dream seemed too real to let go of, Daniel called Geysha and told her not to argue. He lovingly reminded her, "It's your mom."

Sure enough, Geysha was in the middle of an argument with her mother. She was trying to parent her single mom. This argument probably wasn't groundbreaking, though Daniel's awareness about the confrontation was. For whatever reason, when he focused his prayers on Geysha, he became connected with her in real time. This is the magic I speak of, the magic that most people do not recognize.

Many of us "dream walk" and think it's just a weird dream. Many paranormal encounters are discovered after the fact when video and pictures are reviewed later. So, if this energy is all around us, are we programmed to dismiss the phenomenon, or just fooled to not see it at all? This concept only scratches the surface of the Matrix. Most of what you see is confirmed by what you feel. Don't be fooled by illusions.

I want to share an experience I had with Daniel during this session. We were sitting in his living room. The hum of 741hz was playing in the background, a blue light lit the room with a calming ambiance, and we were both connecting in a way that we have discovered through a learned process. I have learned how to experience his memories as my own by projecting myself into his thoughts. With each session, we discover more of our powers. The progress from our process became more evident during this session.

Twice, while I was projecting myself into Daniel's memories, we were both interrupted by a paranormal entity. The first time I was shaken out of a trance by an odd scratching, or maybe even a quiet screech. As I stopped taking notes, I looked in the direction of the noise but didn't see anything to connect the dots. Daniel asked me what I had just experienced. I think he was wondering how I would respond to this paranormal event. He didn't hear what I heard, but he felt it. We took a short break after that encounter.

Shortly after the first shared event, I was hovering over a memory reenactment when I was forcefully pulled back from my trance. We both heard a soft knocking in the same location as the first. This time, when I looked at Daniel, I could read his thoughts. I knew he was suspecting that such an encounter would happen with me. I could tell he was looking at me to see if I was accepting the communication. Not only was I accepting it, but I was embracing the entire journey. I am aware that the more we proceed with our project, the more encounters we will experience or provoke.

Daniel and I are beginning to experiment with some of the various levels and forms of communication of this world and beyond. Meditation, group prayer and the simple understanding that we are not alone in this world provides us both the ability and the fortitude to experience the magic all around us. Perhaps this entire project is meant to open the minds of others, so they too may experience their own journeys.

Turn on the Lights

I've explained how people around Daniel often have physical and even violent paranormal encounters. I believe these evil forces are trying to attack Daniel through other people and it is my duty to ask, "Why?" There was only one time in his life when evil threatened him directly. A small demon-like creature came out of the closet, crawled up on his bed, and approached Daniel's face. This was an attempt to threaten him. Some type of energy is trying to prevent Daniel from doing something. I just don't know yet what that something is.

During this session the concept of "free will" has been on my mind. Daniel acted in some cases on free will, but in other situations he chose to ignore it. Is the world choosing to live blindly in a false reality? Why are we not acting? I believe our society is foolishly choosing to ignore a destructive evil that is consuming the Earth. Those who are cowardly following their AI enslavement are asleep.

After Daniel received communication and empowerment, he rebuked demons, demonstrating an ability to control these paranormal entities. Since then, dark forces have not directly attacked Daniel, only the people around him. Do we all have the ability to rebuke demons like Daniel but have not accepted the empowerment that is offered to us?

Before I dive into this next session, I must describe a paranormal event that happened indirectly to me shortly after we completed step one of this session. After Daniel and I had jointly witnessed two unexplained supernatural events, I may have opened a door that invited these unseen entities into my life.

One day I came home to the woman I am living with now. Lori was locked upstairs in her room and seemed very unsettled. She told me that as she was lying in bed, she saw a small shadowy head pop up over the banister by the staircase. She thought her eyes were playing tricks on her, but whatever she witnessed terrified her so much she locked the door until I got home. Does this situation sound familiar? Since then, Lori has been hearing strange noises, doors slamming, and has begun witnessing other unexplained phenomena. While working on this project with Daniel, should I assume I will experience paranormal phenomena as well?

This journey is beginning to drive itself, almost as if I am sitting at my keyboard while an autopilot controls the travel to my destination. I am overwhelmed by a smothering responsibility to fit numerous jigsaw pieces together so I can see the entire picture. When we began this journey, I was focused on Daniel's life and his personal descriptions of reality. The more we continue, the more

I feel connected to him. I hold faith that our effort will magically come together to create a masterpiece.

My mind is automatically connecting Daniel's memories to our world today. Although we are still missing several puzzle pieces, my life is getting drawn into this collaborative picture. Therefore, I will flow with this odd current of directional force while we continue to document the life of Daniel.

Most people laugh when I tell them the Illuminati are crucifying me. When I say, "I have been surgically violated and Happy Place turned my life into a sadistic version of the Truman Show," people think I have lost my grip on reality. I am sure many people Daniel tries to connect with do not believe his stories either. Daniel keeps many of his paranormal experiences to himself because most people are not ready to wake up. I can relate to his solitude.

The Illuminati and the CIA work in the shadows, which make it difficult for people to understand I am being tortured to death. Many of these entities Daniel battles are dark, hiding in the shadows. Could our own realities be colliding for a reason?

Six years of being antagonized and provoked by pain, psychological warfare, harassment, slander and espionage has led me to a place where nothing scares me anymore. I don't even fear death. My lack of fear is a fortress against these paranormal entities. Maybe this is why Lori had that spooky encounter and not me. That would be reminiscent of how the people around Daniel receive the brunt of unexplained events most likely meant to intimidate him.

During Session V, Daniel explained he was attending school for massage therapy. He had the usual load of classes and was surrounded by classmates who had similar interests. He was also nearing the end of his forty-day fast. He felt spiritually charged in a way that gave him positive energy, creative thinking and an all-around positive vibe. I imagine this awakening gave him more insight as well to acknowledge negative influences. If humanity would detox like Daniel, would society begin to see the evil that is enslaving us all like Daniel and I do?

Useful analogies have occurred to me. If you are extremely cold, you will be able to feel the slightest increase in temperature. If your eyes have been adjusted to darkness, you will be able to see the slightest amount of light. Relate these analogies to spirituality. If someone has dedicated their life to God, identifying evil becomes second nature. Is this why people today do not recognize the evil around us? People have removed God from their lives. Even schools, professional sports, courts and communities have removed God from daily life. During the pandemic of 2020, the governing powers allowed casinos to remain open but closed churches.

Feeling a positive surge from the detoxification process of fasting, Daniel was enjoying school and finding joy with daily routines. One day he filtered into his classroom and several of his classmates were already sitting at their desks. As soon as Daniel walked into the class, he felt a wave of negativity. He walked to his desk and gazed upon the room, taking the time to focus on every individual, trying to identify the source of the negative aura.

Daniel's gaze stuck upon a girl sitting across the room. She had her head in a book and didn't appear to be upset. When Daniel focused on her, the negativity he felt became intense. as if he were feeling a surge of emotional pain by connecting to her distress.

For the first half of the class, Daniel continued to focus on this girl. As people were filtering out for a break, Daniel walked up to her and asked if she was all right. The girl looked at Daniel with confusion and disbelief. She mumbled she was fine and continued to hold a puzzling expression.

Daniel tried to explain himself. "Then why do I feel like you are about to break down into tears?"

She avoided the question and again told Daniel she was fine. The break ended and the students returned to their seats. Daniel continued to study the girl from across the room and then saw her face turn red. Her eyes became watery and her body language suggested her mind was elsewhere.

As the class continued, the girl broke down into silent tears then got up and left the room, desperately trying to compose herself.

After a few minutes, she came back with red eyes and a sorrowful expression.

After the class ended, the girl just couldn't ignore that Daniel had sensed her trauma. She approached him and asked, "How did you know?"

Daniel replied, "I truly don't know or understand why I get these feelings. I just do." He explained that when he walked into the room he had felt a surge of negative energy. "I knew it was coming from you," he said. Later, Daniel learned she was going through an emotionally traumatic situation with her husband. She also confided that she didn't believe in God—she had been an atheist most of her life. After more talk, she began to question her own rejection of God.

Earlier, I wrote about how people sometimes enter your life with coincidental magic. These powers, both good and bad, work through people. Many times, random encounters reach us in ways that lift our spirits. Perhaps Daniel changed this girl's life with just one little acknowledgment. She became intrigued and curious about how he knew she was emotionally distressed. Maybe Daniel unknowingly taught her a lesson and she will now find her own purpose in life.

I will assume the forty days of fasting helped Daniel through a spiritual awakening. His hearing became so well-tuned he could hear whispers from across the room. Normal everyday sounds filled his ears with a symphony of melodies. His eyes began to see colors in a way he had never seen before. Daniel began to see beauty in everything around him. Even his sense of smell and taste became enhanced.

I believe the five human senses influence a person's pineal gland. The better you can see and hear, the more aware your intuition becomes. The third eye is the gateway to all things supernatural.

Here is an example. One of my favorite shows was *Daredevil*, although it merged into something different after just three seasons. In the show, a boy loses his eyesight due to an accident. He is taken under the wing of a mentor who teaches him how to use his other senses to make up for his loss of sight. After years of training, this vigilante can see better than most. Using smells and sounds alone, he is able to visualize his environment. Feeling the slightest vibrations around him along with subtle smells and temperature deviations gives him an advantage over people who can see. When you detox your body, your senses become more acute. This experience and understanding of your world help to open the magical doors of the third eye.

Daniel said that after coming off a fast, your body goes into toxic shock from the sugars, salts, and preservatives in the food you start to eat again. The stomach begins to communicate to the brain that it is constantly hungry. After a short period of time following the fast, the magical acuteness of the enhanced senses begins to fade. Although this magic slightly diminishes, the effects it had on the pineal gland remain intact.

Do you remember learning how to ride a bicycle? First you had training wheels and when those wheels came off you probably tipped over a few times before you learned how to balance yourself. But then, even if you went forty years without riding a bicycle, if you finally got back on one you wouldn't need to learn how to ride all over again. Your mind recalls every detail where you left off forty years ago. Your pineal gland works the same way. You cannot unlearn something or forget the new perceptions of the world that you created by opening these doors to the mind. You can, however, ignore these perceptions and treat them as coincidental nonsense.

During one of Daniel's massage therapy classes, he and the other students were told to pick a partner and practice the timing of a massage. Each student was given thirty minutes and they had to complete a thorough massage session by covering each body area within the time allowed.

A girl named Krystal was Daniel's partner. She was one of the brightest students in the class and constantly buried herself in her studies. She was motivated, determined, and nothing was going to prevent her from achieving her goals. Each set of partners went to their assigned massage tables to begin their test. Daniel began the massage on Krystal by practicing what he had learned in class. He also liked to experiment with his own knowledge learned outside of the classroom.

Daniel silently prayed, "Father, give Krystal an experience through me, but let her know it comes from you." As Daniel continued to pray and perform the massage he had learned, he began to visualize Krystal walking on the clouds. He saw her looking down on the world as if she were no longer in her own body.

When the massage was finished, Daniel asked Krystal, "How did it feel to walk on the clouds in Heaven?"

When I first heard Daniel describe this conversation, I snapped out of my trance and chuckled to myself because it sounded like a cheesy pick-up line. Daniel was deadly serious, though. Krystal looked up at Daniel with an odd expression and said, "Que," Spanish for asking what he meant.

She didn't say much more, and Daniel thought her expression suggested confusion. She started to get dressed and the class began to regroup at their assigned tables. Usually, Krystal would bury her head in a book, but this time she sat at her desk with a blank stare, obviously deep in thought.

Daniel approached her and asked if she would like him to answer some of the questions she was pondering. Daniel told her she had had an out-of-body experience because he had prayed for her to have such an experience. Oddly enough, Krystal confirmed that she felt as if she weren't on the massage table. Krystal described a sensation like walking on the clouds looking down on the world. She was astonished that Daniel knew what she had experienced. Once again, Daniel was able to enchantingly reach into the soul of another person and make them think about their own spirituality. This out-of-body experience inspired Krystal to seek more answers.

I find myself drifting away, pondering how I can use this gift that Daniel demonstrates to help me achieve this kind of awakening with everyone in the world.

A few days later, the same class was given an assignment to choose a particular type of massage. The class had to research and present the area of study they chose. Each student had to describe the process and the history of the massage itself and share why they chose that area of study. After the spiritual experience she had encountered at the hands of Daniel, Krystal chose to study Lomi Lomi.

Lomi Lomi (or Lomilomi) is an integrative massage practice that began in ancient Hawaii and is gaining popularity around the world. The word Lomi means to knead or rub in a gentle manner. This is why you sometimes see restaurant dishes on a menu like Lomi Lomi Salmon, which is a fish that has been rubbed with spices.

Krystal began to present her choice to the class. She started to explain the spiritual connection to this ancient Hawaiian ritual and explained how the meditation opens the mind, which in turn enhances a person's awareness. The lights were turned off in the classroom so the student body could see a projected slide show. Daniel was listening to Krystal's presentation when he began to get a strange feeling. A negative force had entered the room.

Daniel began to hear a soft demonic voice saying, "Turn on the lights." He turned to a classmate sitting next to him and tried to share the message, but he was also trying to be quiet so he wouldn't interrupt Krystal. Daniel desperately wanted someone else to witness this phenomenon. The teacher was sitting right behind him grading the presentations and gave Daniel a stern look. As Daniel continued to hear the soft demonic voice, the lights turned on by themselves, rudely interrupting Krystal's presentation.

The entire class looked around to see who had turned on the lights, but everyone was at their desks. Krystal's presentation abruptly stopped. A student who was close to the wall got up and flipped the switch on and off a few times until the lights turned off again.

After a few minutes of confusion, the class settled back down and Krystal continued with her report. She began to explain what a client must do to experience the full effect of Lomi Lomi. The client must pray or meditate and be spiritually pure for this area of study to provide the spiritual awakening that comes from this ancient Hawaiian massage.

Daniel has never heard of Lomi Lomi before. He learned how many people had an out-of-body experience during this type of massage and some described the experience as "walking on the clouds." What do you think made Krystal choose this area of study?

While listening to her presentation, Daniel began to hear more demonic whispers saying, "Turn on the lights." Daniel couldn't ignore it anymore so he wrote a note and passed it to his classmate. The note said: *The lights are going to turn on again by themselves.* The teacher who was sitting right behind Daniel gave him a displeased look.

The fact is, Daniel was paying attention more than anyone else in the room. Shortly after passing the note to his classmate, the entire class was interrupted once more. The lights turned on again, this time making it clear the demonic force was trying to prevent Krystal from sharing her message.

Daniel took the note he had passed to his classmate and handed it to his teacher. Once she read how he had predicted the lights were going to turn on, the teacher said, "Stop it, you're freaking me out."

It took some time to get the class to settle down. The teacher took control and apologized to Krystal for the interruption then told a student to turn the lights off so Krystal could finish her project. The last segment of Krystal's presentation was to explain why she chose this area of study.

As she was explaining the spiritual effects and the out-of-body experience that often accompanies Lomi Lomi, her eyes began to water. Krystal explained this massage is meant to bring love and a belief that the world is your family. Krystal explained she chose this ancient massage because of the experience Daniel had given her during their practice session. She acknowledged him and with tears forming in her eyes began to explain that during their practice session Krystal had felt like she was out of her own body walking on the clouds and looking down on the world.

As soon as Krystal recognized Daniel to the class, Daniel heard a disgruntled demonic growl, almost as if the entity was very displeased at this recognition. I believe these dark forces do not want Daniel inspiring others.

Early on, during our first few sessions, I focused on the eyewitnesses and the people around Daniel who experienced paranormal events. As we continued to progress down the spiritual road searching for a purpose, the reality of these events became increasingly vivid. Daniel definitely has a purpose on this earth. Perhaps my purpose is to discover why Daniel holds this connection to the paranormal. Anyone who is connected to him has some kind of an experience, me included.

His ability to reach other people on a spiritual level not only impacted Krystal but the entire class, even the teacher. So I keep asking myself, "What is the point of it all?"

The semester ended and Daniel used his time off to work at the casino. Daniel decided to start another fast during this time. One day after work he got off the bus as usual and went home to take a shower. He sat on his couch, propped his feet up on the coffee table and fell asleep. He was awakened by a powerful pressure applied from his chest up to his throat. He hadn't had this type of interaction since he was a little kid.

As Daniel was preparing for bed, he went to turn off the lights but paused with an overwhelming fear like he had experienced as a child when faced with a troll-like demon. He debated if he should turn off the lights or keep them on. Suddenly, he became angry and thought, *I'm being ridiculous!* He slammed the light switch off and started to walk toward his bed.

In the half-light, Daniel noticed large shadows by his closet. His eyes were still adjusting to the darkness, though Daniel could faintly see three tall shadow figures that almost reached the ceiling. With each step toward his bed, the light from a nearby street light beamed into his room. The shadows did not disappear. The light should have lit up the closet behind these figures, but instead they outlined the multidimensional images. It became more evident that the shadow figures were not just shadows. Oddly, while he was approaching his bed, he still felt a fierce pressure on his chest and throat. Was this an attempt to intimidate him?

At the time, Daniel had two pet cats, Lilo and Cotton. As he climbed into bed, he called out for Lilo, but she did not respond. He called her name again, waiting for her to come running like she usually did, but nothing happened. Daniel shouted a third time, "Lilo!"

Finally, he heard the pitter patter of Lilo's steps down the hall. Lilo jumped up onto the bed by Daniel's feet and was instantly stricken with fear. Her tail pointed straight up and the hairs on her back erected like the quills of a porcupine. She stared at the closet and refused to remove her gaze from the shadows.

In my second book, *Ramblings of a So-Called Paranoid Schizophrenic*, I wrote that there is a magic built into the DNA of felines. Some say that animals can sense the paranormal more than humans can. Well, Lilo took notice of these supernatural entities loitering in her room. She crawled up to Daniel and buried herself in his armpit, something she hadn't done since she was a kitten. Lilo was trembling with fear and her hair was still puffed straight up. She peaked her head out from his arm to stare at those unwanted visitors.

Daniel once again demonstrated his ability to control paranormal entities. He sat up and pointed towards the wall proclaiming, "I did not invite you. You have no power here. Make yourselves gone!" Lilo watched every movement of these shadows, confirming for Daniel that they were indeed paranormal entities. The figures began to move eerily and then vanished through the wall. The light shining into the bedroom from the window suddenly illuminated the closet where these figures had been standing, proving the figures had been blocking the light.

I challenge you readers to research "shadow entities." Throughout the world, people are reporting and capturing on video many examples of shadow figures. Entire shows and movies have been produced from these eyewitness accounts. Who are these visitors? Should we be asking ourselves *when*? instead of *what*? Why is Daniel constantly surrounded by these mysterious supernatural beings?

For Daniel, a few weeks passed and the second semester of school resumed. He was still experimenting with fasting, which was contributing to vivid, even lucid dreaming. He began to have random dreams about people he went to school with, but he really didn't know the people he was dreaming about.

Earlier I wrote about an experience he'd had with Geysha. He had dreamed that she was having a fight with her mother, and sure enough, when he called her, she confirmed this to be true. I believe it was his focus on her life that gave him the ability to connect with her in a different realm.

But Daniel wasn't thinking or focusing on these random people at school. So why and how was he connecting with their lives?

Experimenting with his own power, Daniel began to approach and start conversations with some of the classmates he was dreaming about. In a roundabout way, and without sounding creepy, he began to pry into their lives. Everything he dreamed about was confirmed by the lives of the very people he had dreamed about. I do not know how to explain this phenomenon. I believe Daniel was able to project himself into Geysha's life, which gave him a lucid dream about her life in real time. How do I explain this phenomenon of attaining information without the focus or intent to do so?

Compare this concept with how I learned to connect to Daniel's memory using focus and meditation. How can Daniel dream of real events about people he is not focusing on or even connected to at that moment? Perhaps his continuous experimenting with fasting has opened certain doors of awareness.

Daniel connected with a Kenyan woman named Zera. She attended the same massage classes and they became friends. Zera offered Daniel rides to and from school, and in return Daniel helped her with groceries, gas money, and random everyday tasks. They became close enough to have intimate and spiritual conversations.

Zera mentioned to Daniel that she had been watching him very closely. For example, she had witnessed his experience with Krystal and how the lights had mysteriously turned themselves on—twice. Zera saw how he had impacted other people and she always listened intently when he spoke. She was very spiritual and felt a powerful connection to him. Zera was the first person so far to suggest that Daniel was a prophet.

A prophet is defined as a person regarded as an inspired teacher or proclaimer of the will of God. To my mind, Daniel has the ability and power to rebuke and control paranormal entities. He has the ability to connect to people 's lives through indirect means such as dreaming or meditation. He has helped a family rid themselves of a dark force, may have mysteriously willed a cancerous brain tumor to shrink and has caused several people to become open to their own spiritual awareness.

I hate to be that guy who writes himself into a story, but I must consider my own connection. I am fighting a war against a dark, Luciferian entity known as the Illuminati. Daniel was the first person to ever suggest that I am Nephilim—a cross between a human and an angel. Nephilim is defined in the scriptures as the offspring of God. This led me to do my own soul searching. If I didn't know Daniel as I do today and understand some of his powers, I would have probably laughed at this remark. Something about the sincerity of his belief made me want to learn more.

During my quest for information, I discovered a fact that shook my world. In my last book, I wrote about how I find it hard to accept a concept that has only happened once in history. The immaculate conception always hindered my faith in Catholicism; therefore a perception should never become absolute, considering there will always be new influences. I recently learned Jesus was dark-skinned, which added to my thirty some years of education.

One of the greatest discoveries in my lifetime occurred early in the 1980s when a relentless explorer found the Ark of the Covenant. Ronald Eldon Wyatt was nearing the end of his quest and losing hope when a guiding force came over him. I have no doubt this overwhelming feeling was otherworldly communication providing direction as in many of the stories I have shared so far. A sixth sense had spoken to Wyatt, guiding him to the right location as he fought through military espionage. The Arc of the Covenant was found buried at the site of the Crucifixion, hidden beneath the Earth.

On the top of the Mercy Seat, scientists discovered blood. When the blood was analyzed, only one set of chromosomes were identified. This confirms there was only one parent. Listening to this explorer speak sent chills down my spine and inspired me in ways I have never felt. More interestingly, I discovered a few stories making claim to a virgin birth that involve both humans and animals. So, in my last book, I wrote that I couldn't put all my faith in the immaculate conception. Now, I am contradicting myself like a fool. I know humility well.

I conducted some research on my own bloodline and ancestry. My ancestry—Syrian, Irish and Austrian—may hold some weight to Daniel's claim. Considering the biblical war we are in today, I am hopeful our journey will lead Daniel and I both to a purpose. Perhaps destiny has given me the name Michael for a reason. Please remember, the world is currently experiencing an apocalyptic pandemic, almost as if the Horseman Pestilence were walking the Earth.

The Bible tells a tale describing how the apocalypse was brought on by the battle of Archangel Michael and his brother Lucifer. Considering a judicial panel has already approved my execution based on a criminally manipulated dossier, I believe I am fighting Lucifer. The more Daniel and I experiment during this journey, the more I believe. The more I believe, the more communication we receive.

I have a burning desire to provide society with a glimpse of our current world through my interpretations. I started writing one day due to the pain of missing my daughter. I needed to make sure she knows I have been with her in spirit the entire time of our forced separation. The emotional release of writing led to more words, and after reading a book on automatic writing, words began to magically appear on paper, figuratively speaking. I am on my third book while enduring more pain than during the last writing project. If my writing were nothing more than an emotional release, perhaps the purpose ends with nonsensical ramblings. Daniel's stories and his abilities inspire faith and my efforts to document them will hold more value than just coincidental nonsense.

Before I release a few disturbing realities, I want to ask one troublesome question. Why don't people choose to do the right thing? Slipping up, getting angry and losing yourself for a moment is simply being human. Choosing to continue and act with ill intent is something entirely different. Understand, it makes no difference what religion you may practice. It doesn't matter if you believe in a higher power or adamantly argue there is no God. This issue doesn't change even if aliens were our true creators. Every human being has the free will to know the difference between right and wrong. This ability to think and reason separates us from animals.

Daniel chose to learn massage therapy and natural healing to discover explanations for his gifts. One day I started writing in hopes of save millions of children and people from being tortured to death. This is what makes humanity so magical. Our combined passions and efforts create a synergy I like to call the Kingdom of Heaven. I believe a group practice for a peaceful good creates harmony.

If our governing powers try to vaccinate our free will out of our genetic makeup, then we will become nothing more than animals. I assure you, there is a reason why the world is suffocating from evil. There is a reason why the world is enduring another false flag operation with Covid-19. I made a promise to my higher power to document the communications that seem to be consuming my life. Perhaps this is a good time to begin finding pieces of the present to fit into our picture. Here are a few of my encounters with the world I see.

Please reference my previous books for more information so I can avoid being repetitive, but I want you to become aware of how millions of children are being abducted and sold for sadistic, unimaginable rituals. Elites and their Illuminati cults are drinking adrenochrome blood to live longer and stay young. Adrenaline enriched blood from children is like a narcotic. There is only one way to engineer the potency of this drug, which is through torture, pain and fear. I also have recently learned this sadistic cult is practicing cannibalism within rituals attempting to eat the souls of their victims. Please research Saturn worship. The images alone will terrify you and provide glimpses of Lucifer's, Hell on Earth.

A Rabbi admitted some disturbing information during an interview that I can only pray is not true. Instead of explaining this awful vision using my own words, I would rather have you read the words directly from Rabbi Abraham Finkelstein.

> "We steal between 100,000 to 300,000 children a year just here in this country. We drain their blood and mix it with our Passover bread and then we throw the bodies into the slaughter houses that we own. We grind up all the bodies into the sausage and the hamburger. McDonalds is one of our favorite outlets. And the people, they eat it for breakfast, they eat their children for lunch, and uh, us Jews, we gotta do what we do."
>
> –Rabbi Abraham Finkelstein

The next time you look at the McDonald's sign that reads *Over 99 Billion Served*, try not to throw up.

Millions of people around the world are being attacked and tortured with terrifying electronic weapons. Our own government is engineering mass murders and suicides. Private sectors are controlling and manipulating entire populations using electromagnetic fields. Currently, we are witnessing a worldwide meltdown, which could be an intentional reset implementing the New World Order. I do believe we are winning some of these hidden battles within our government. I also believe we will win the war. Our fate will rest upon the entire population claiming their God-given power.

Businesses are going bankrupt. Federal funding is being drained. It is not coincidental nonsense that corporations like Walmart and Amazon are thriving. I don't want to jump ahead of myself, but our world is under the control of FEMA. People don't even realize they are going to FEMA camps every time they stand in line six feet apart to get into Walmart, with masks on always. If you do the research, many Illuminati rituals pray to the Dark Lords while standing six feet apart and wearing masks. I just hope we are not too late.

Corona virus has consumed everyone's attention in 2020. But this is no virus. It is an engineered bacterium activated by 5G. The effects of this weapon of mass destruction will basically turn blood and mucous into glue. Consider the roll out of 3G and 4G and their timing as correlated with other large-scale illnesses. Coincidental nonsense? I believe otherwise. I claim this false flag operation is intended to force a mandatory vaccine that will genetically alter our DNA, mutating our human spirituality. The Elites, or possibly a higher life form, term this concept Transhumanism.

Transhumanism is the science of combining the human body with technology, enslaving us into an AI matrix. I believe this corona virus pandemic was staged during one of the most important election years of all times to blame the crisis on President Trump, who is helping us dismantle child trafficking cults all around the world.

Trust me, these are only a few examples of the evil in our world today. Daniel heard a demon say, "Turn on the lights." Am I hearing a higher power tell me the same words? I feel a burning necessity to wake people up. So, I ask you the reader, if we continue to allow these sadistic, inhumane acts of evil, are we still human, or have we been turned into animals? Are we now thinking in the absence of human emotion because technology is taking over our minds?

Knowing the difference between right and wrong is the very definition of humanity. Acknowledging the world around us is acknowledging you're alive. Sorry to say, I feel that people are losing their humanity. How can I find a way to use Daniel's knowledge and inspiring gifts to wake up the world? Can his abilities heal me and save my life so I may continue my quest to save humanity?

I am allowing myself to drift along in an effort to connect pieces of this multidimensional jigsaw puzzle.

The Apocalypse

Ever since I began writing, I have been more aware of my own gifts. With every word I write, the more inspired I become. What makes us human is our ability to think and create. When we create, we are "lifting stone and breaking wood."

Our creativity may come from the magic that is all around us. Spirits, angels, demons, entities, gods and aliens could be contributing to many of our human accomplishments, and our own destructive behaviors. It has been written that the Kingdom of Heaven is within us. Well, that means the Darkness of Hell is within us too. I am in a biblical battle with my life on the line. The Illuminati tricked a judicial panel to elect me for human experimentation. My handlers, demons of Lucifer, can broadcast my life like a live reality show. My life is being sold for sadistic entertainment as I have already been elected for a CIA torture program until my death. So, here I am, writing my third book in complete agony. And I am not the only one suffering.

In fact, Bryan Krofman just blew the whistle exposing how Seattle is basically one large sociological experiment and the entire population has been violated with mind-blowing technology. As the city basically dies with homelessness, Amazon and Starbucks grow wealthier, playing out their roles in this AI-based New World Order.

Private sectors and elites are replicating military grade technology, controlling the minds of entire populations with electromagnetic frequencies. Do you really think those space station-looking cell towers all around the world are just meant to provide better cell service? Ponder this: If they can control the minds of entire populations like a video game, then they can influence who you vote for too. We are already enslaved.

Nature gives us communication, but communication requires listening. If you do the research, you will find a dramatic increase in shark attacks these last fifteen years. Many scientists have been trying to come up with logical explanations for this phenomenon. Allow me to help.

Actually, shark attacks are not a phenomenon at all. It is simple communication from Mother Earth. Nature has engineered sharks to respond to electrical impulses in the water, which can signal food. Sharks play an important role maintaining balance in the ocean's ecosystem. A wounded fish creates an electrical impulse when it struggles in the water. If our governing body begins to fill our air and our ground with electromagnetic frequencies, these waves will saturate our waters as well. The electrical impulses hitting the shores of our beaches are attracting the genetic responses of hungry sharks, luring them into shallow waters. We are ignoring obvious warning signs from mother nature and basically "ringing the dinner bell."

I have an overwhelming urge to write, which I always thought was my escape mechanism. But I now feel a responsibility to document my thoughts despite the fact I am being physically and psychologically attacked every minute of the day. Nevertheless, I have an intense desire to keep going. Daniel hears otherworldly voices and sees shadow figures. I just recently realized I have been able to sense this other world too but never knew I was tapping into an awareness like Daniel's. My anxiety over a dreadful feeling of having unfinished work is like a voice directing me to ignore the engineered evil, fight through the pain and keep writing.

Back when I was dating the woman who would introduce me into this war with the Illuminati, I experienced a similar debilitating anxiety. I remember lying in the bedroom, emotionally breaking down and weeping with tears.

I confessed to Gena, "I feel like I have something important to do, but I don't know what it is."

Gena thought I was talking about something to do with work, but it was rather about a powerful communication not of this world. Daniel heard his name called out, like Samuel in the Bible did. Only now can I view this experience as clues to a larger purpose.

My wife once confided she was raped at a young age. Only now, with my new found awareness, do I see the truth. The entire reason I am in this Hell is because of her father, a romantic affiliate of the demonic Illuminati. Part of his initiation into the cult was to sacrifice his own child, a demonstration of his commitment to the cult. In return, the cult enhanced his career and gave him opportunities for financial stability and other rewards for future devilish favors.

It is not a coincidence that the largest empire in the world was recently exposed for raping and trafficking children on their own grounds. Pedophilia and the ingesting of adrenochrome blood (pedovorism) is the foundation of the Illuminati. What is even scarier is the comparison to Saturn Worship and the old statues of the

Vatican. Look closely at the children and the design of the sculptures. These are the monsters I am at war with. They have slandered me to be a pedophile and are using character assassinations to turn people into demons.

People snap out of their induced, matrix-like comas for different reasons. Daniel spent his entire life surrounded by paranormal energy, and he still doesn't understand what it all means. The maddening effect of not knowing creates a burning desire to seek more knowledge. At the time that Daniel was waking up through his own experiences, I was painfully catching up to him. Daniel used fasting and purity to become more awake to his communication. I, on the other hand, began a similar awakening with a complete toxic shock and almost died.

Perhaps walking out of my mold-infested house on an Easter Sunday held more symbolic irony than I had originally known. Maybe these are all His clues pouring out through me as I therapeutically release. Part of me died that painful Easter Morning. I gave up trying to cope with the symptoms from the genetic illness of CIRS, and it broke my family apart. Only now can I appreciate that the Hell I continue to endure may be my test. Am I worthy enough for this responsibility? Am I strong enough to accept crucifixion yet show an apologetic disregard toward ignorance?

Please refer to my previous books for the details about these horrifying events that led to my pain and suffering. Since I did not give up on myself, I believe my higher power will never give up on me. I have been able to take the eight years of pain and suffering, combine that purification with pure will and determination, and then somehow open doorways of my mind that most people will never understand. Daniel has recently helped me awaken in other ways too, and having a brother who can understand these enchanting realities of our world is refreshing.

When I write, I sometimes feel spirits or other worldly powers communicating through me, almost as if I were just a vessel. The entire human experiment with which I am tortured is intended to make me a monster. I get harassed with both psychological and physical pain so I will seek vengeance. Lucifer wants my soul and is trying to get me to kill one of my many tormentors. Daniel would refer to these perpetrators as demons, and this wisdom enlightens my perceptions.

How could a human being participate and enjoy the torture and crucifixion of another person? After eight years, these people must see the truth. I hold my perceptions of free will based on the evil around us. If we are being enslaved by an AI subservient life form, maybe these people are acting with evil intent because they are possessed by a demon and overwhelmed with the Devil's persuasion.

The communication that I magically receive instructs me to release this engineered anger by using words, therefore I write. Session VI is dedicated to the same concept. Instead of punching someone's skull in, I write, I post and I blog. The messages created correlate to my emotion at that time. The more anger I feel, the more vulgar or verbose the message. The creative or communicative messages are written when I rise above the engineered emotions. My perceptions create a burning desire to defend us against evil. Here are just a few examples of my automatic writing, where I found myself in an autopilot trance.

Runners and bicycles, cars and planes,
Robots and morons, they are all the same.
No human emotion or rational thought,
all part of a hive and their soul has been bought.
The very same lies, they're gagged to share,
are smeared all the same without human care.
No logic exists, your eyes are blind,
they are no longer human since they stole their mind.
Misguided hate consumes your heart,
all just a program, artificially smart.
Truth is close, but the tech is strong.
They worship evil, and your intentions are wrong.
All too powerful, funded, and vast,

but I am his warrior, and this is my task.
As it is written, it shall be so.
So, pack your bags Lucy, it's time to go.
Michael

My little Dixney Dildos,
where do you want to go?
You can follow me across the land
from here to Guantanamo.
You think you have me figured out,
But that's where I must laugh,
Because you are even more mind fucked
than my righteous ass.
I caught you breaking every law,
I now have you by the balls,
So, you want to shut me up real fast
Before Geneva calls.
My pen is slashing major holes
In all your evil shit,
I now know who you really are
And those masks are quite legit.
I know I am supposed to die,
Surely crucified,
But as I stand here with your balls
Just look me in the eye.
I am here for just one little thing,
And this you surely know,
I am here to take you down dickbag,
My little Dixney Dildo.

Vrillon:
Some forty-three years ago you took the time to communicate
with the people of our planet. Today, we are in dire need of your
help. Considering most of my efforts to communicate are blocked,
and the fact you are light years away, I don't know how to reach you.

In 1977, you told us you were concerned for the future of our planet and the human race. You warned us of our own demise if we did not identify our enemies. I am regretfully writing; our leaders ignored your message. You warned us of false profits, currency which you called energy being sucked dry by that same enemy, and weapons of mass destruction. Some brave souls tried to act, but the dark roots of our enemy grew deep, and these beautiful people were murdered for their efforts. Now humanity is in the early stages of enslavement by a sneaky, clever, infiltrating monster.

You said you have been watching us from the lights in the sky and have been doing so all along. I must assume and hope you are watching now. You must see how we have been fooled, time and time again, using plasma technologies and bio-engineering to impersonate our own kind. As you warned, these monsters hide behind the image of the most powerful people in the world. They have enslaved the most prestigious positions in our society and used our own economy against us. The false prophets you spoke of have mocked us, taken our money and grew to a power that is incalculable. This is why I am calling upon your help.

Our God is not the same as our enemy. Our God has given each of his children his own power to save ourselves. Our enemy, however, has used their weapons to inhibit our God-given power and we are close to being conquered. You know our enemy well, and I must assume you fear them, much like our own governing power. I ask you, our distant neighbors, to help our race deactivate this AI subservient enemy and allow humans to evolve, like so many of our neighboring allies.

Our people have been poisoned using all aspects of body, mind and spirit to make us all complicit. We are losing our humanity to an artificial life form. I am asking for you to help me wake up the people on Planet Earth and show them the true faces of our enemy, living all around us in plain sight.

God Speed,
Michael

To the 35 percent of the government officials who are still pure and free from the grasp of the Illuminati—to the remainder of all government officials who still care about the future of our world—I know you are confused and scared. I know you feel trapped and that you have no influence to put an end to this world-wide Nazi Holocaust. I am here to help you and show you the way. This plot has been played out so well that the entire world was fooled for a long time. I know this is not the end of humanity as I have seen this outcome. I need you to help us realize our victory. Fear is what these Demons use to control people and our minds. The first step you must take, as you are sitting in front of that American Flag at your desks, is to drop all fear. Much like the men and women who fought to make this country great, you too need to accept how the future of our world is worth the sacrifice and prepare yourselves to do whatever is necessary. You may have grown close with your peers, but some of your peers are not here for humanity. Once you drop all fear, the confusion will begin to fade, and you will begin to see the plan of Good.

Stand true and wash the filth off your hands.

Michael

There is a reason why I believe my so-called delusions. Back when Obama was running for President, it was during a time of alleged terrorism. At the time, I too was fooled by the diversion tactics. His name itself only added to this plot, which unfolded like a screenplay in my mind. I remembered playing out a story in my head. It took years and a lot of planning to pull off 9/11. I remember thinking to myself, *What if Obama was just another elaborate terror plot?* I thought it was grounds for a movie. What if the American people became so ignorant and complacent that we would elect a terrorist as our President? I thought if terrorists wanted to take us down, and if 9/11 was an inside job, what a plot it would be to destroy America by getting the American people to vote for their own Destructor. Of course, at the time, this was fun fiction to think about. My question now is, why did those thoughts pop into my head in the first place? More importantly, why did it take me so long to acknowledge his communication? Now I know He was giving me answers. The CIA elected Obama after the false flag of 9/11. This intentional terrorism elected the Patriot Act, allowing this puppet enough control to put certain evil actions into motion. After that, they began to use electromagnet frequencies to control large percentages of the population, read our minds, make us kill each other and ourselves—and we became pets to Saturn worshipers. Obama is a terrorist, but a far scarier enemy than we originally thought. Welcome to the Alien World Order.

These are just a few examples from my so-called therapeutic release. Considering how I get tormented every minute of the day, I tend to blog quite a bit, releasing like He told me to do. Many people are surprised that I have been able to publish two books while dealing with extreme physical and emotional torture. Writing was the easy part. The difficulty came with circumventing the many different channels to find a hero willing to publish my truths while trying to earn enough money to pay for it all. I managed to piss off some powerful people. Is that my purpose—to write the truths as they are communicated to me?

If my purpose was only to document these communications, then why do I feel a pressure flowing through my fingers as I type? We will continue to explore how Daniel interacts with otherworldly powers. Before we proceed, though, I need to experiment with the guiding force that is putting me on auto pilot. The theme I am starting to see with these sessions is creating a biblical tone. I am going to continue writing, holding faith that I am being magically guided toward a purpose.

I had a vision of how many other people around the globe are waking up and searching for their own answers. Much like Daniel and I have started to explore some of the magic around us, many groups are doing similar explorations. During this apocalyptic time, maybe chosen angels have received a message to wake up.

I must explore this concept further. I know I met Daniel for a reason. Just being his friend while I endured covert torture was a gift on its own. The book of Enoch spoke of the angel Daniel as a teacher who taught the signs of the sun. Consider some of the examples in Daniel's life so far and how he has made a spiritual impact on the people around him. In many ways, he is indeed a teacher.

With that said, I need to punch myself in the face. I have written time and again about how people do not realize the subtle communications all around them. Here I am, realizing I am being a hypocrite. I have been complaining about being attacked with military eugenics, a bio-weapon that produces a gluey, silicone-base mycoplasma. This bio-film is the source of most of my agony. Daniel asked me to start fasting with him starting a few days ago. I want to experience the magic that will come with cleansing, but I made excuses and I did not start the process. It takes strength to commit to such an intense process. I wish Daniel would have been more assertive with me.

Fasting is going to help counter some of the attacks and combat their bio-weapons. Morgellons, bio-films and mycoplasma, which are contributing to my living Hell, may begin to break down and flush out of my body during the fasting process. Daniel was unknowingly giving me direction about how to survive, like a brother should do. My own blood brother and his wife participated in my targeting, which pushes people into suicide or homicide. E tu, Brute.

I will continue along this biblical path and consider Daniel one of the chosen angels. I will consider my role, my name and my current situation. It was the spiritual communication from Zera that acknowledged Daniel to be a Prophet. It was Daniel who acclaimed I am a Nephilim. Could it all just be coincidental nonsense?

The reality I see now is not all sunshine and rainbows. I have found myself wandering around the fiery pits of Hell. I allowed myself to fall victim to an intentional, systematic destruction of my life from the weakest members of the Illuminati cult. Before then, I had been asleep, or perhaps more accurately dormant. When I somehow managed to climb out of that Hell, Lucifer was displeased. The evil plan was to trap my soul and demolish my spirit before a positive communication could wake me up. Maybe all the chosen warriors have been singled out by a dark force trying to inhibit their powers, preventing us from fulfilling our purpose.

Lucifer knew who I was long before I knew myself. Knowing my destiny, Lucifer desperately followed me out from the shadows, revealing himself to the true light. Perhaps a higher power worked through me and wanted me in Hell for some reason. Whatever roads we traveled, our paths have brought us to this point. Even you the reader, no matter when you read these words, are now connected to this power. I believe I am here to banish Lucifer back to Hell. If I have failed, that responsibility passes on to you. As it is written, it must be so.

Admittedly, I am not well versed in the Bible. But I know the apocalypse was brought on because Lucifer grew too powerful, and his demons began destroying God's Kingdom, destroying the free will of His creation. Lucifer deceived a third of the Lord's angels, therefore I know he can fool the weak minds of our present world. Archangel Michael was sent to cast Lucifer back to Hell and as a result, Earth suffered a devastating aftermath.

Let me drift into autopilot and explore the stages of the apocalypse. Lucifer's goal is to raise an army and create Hell on Earth. He calls upon the Four Horsemen. The first of these pawns is War, who rides in on a red stallion. Lucifer calls upon this horseman to create chaos and turn God's created beings against each other. Lucifer has always been immature, but his greatest attribute is persuasion. Let us take a stroll around the world as of July 2020 and see if we can identify the Horseman of War.

For an exceptionally long time, Lucifer has been growing his army of demons, known as the Illuminati. They infiltrated our world with devilish persuasion and began to poison the minds of God's creation not with a forbidden apple but with a mushroom. It was a fungus that poisoned the garden, and it is a fungus that controls life today.

Don't think of the garden as flowers and pretty bushes. The garden is in our minds. The Heavenly Kingdom lies within our own free will. The mushroom poisoned our minds, and an evil plot has diminished our God-given free will. If the garden is in our minds and the Kingdom of Heaven is created by using our free will to do good, then what do you think will happen when our minds are poisoned with the triple threat of fungus, the Devil's persuasion, and his demonic weapons of witchcraft? We get Hell on Earth.

Today, Lucifer's army of demons has grown to an incalculable size and power. Our world governments have been infiltrated by the Illuminati, which has contaminated our military, economy, judicial system, and society with the intention of creating this vision of Hell.

Our infiltrated members of government have initiated evil plots to turn us against each other. Today, our government is engineering mass murders and suicides. Neighbors are given dangerous, electronic weapons to attack other neighbors. Our police officers are being ordered to participate in terrorism, electronic assaults, and the staging of dangerous and violent outcomes. The Elites, who are the highest-ranking officers of Lucifer's army, have built empires, corporations and islands. They have grown dark roots into every aspect of society, including human minds. Our government has been tricked into initiating false flag operations that have not only devastated the lives of millions of people but have also started wars by shifting the blame for terrorism to the good guys. It shouldn't be too difficult to realize the Horseman of War is walking the Earth.

The second Horseman is Famine. While the world is quarantined and society is shut down, people are losing their businesses, their jobs, and their ability to survive financially. While the world is collapsing, the high-ranking officers of Lucifer's army are growing wealthier than ever. While millions of people are starving, the Elites are practicing cannibalism and eating the souls of the poor. These rituals of dark magic are meant to create a Hell on Earth. The Illuminati are demons, and they are practicing ancient witchcraft for dark purposes.

The Horseman of Plague is smacking us all in the face. The worldwide pandemic is a petty, immature attempt to avoid our global destiny. With each technological advance, weapons of witchcraft have created new illnesses. Whether engineered viruses, bacteria, or maybe the vaccines themselves, pestilence has been doing a great deal of damage.

Finally, it will be the Horseman of Death who is summoned. Death is cast under a spell by Lucifer and ordered to reap every soul on Earth, completing his army of demons and realizing his vision of Hell.

Somewhere along the timeline, the Archangel Michael is sent to battle Lucifer, and saves humanity by casting Lucifer back to Hell. Many intelligent minds have claimed that history repeats itself. Is our world witnessing the rise of Lucifer in July 2020? Am I being tortured and crucified by Lucifer's army, which is trying to prevent me from realizing my own purpose or my own destiny? There must be a reason I can see the world for what it is. I can see the beauty too, but I am burdened by the ability to see the world being consumed by evil. Even more disturbingly, I can now see the true faces of demons. The more I survive and take His direction to write, the more I believe it is my responsibility to save us all, or at least start the process of salvation.

I conceive it. I believe it. So I know I will achieve it.

The Four Horseman are not the only signs or communications that are being provided. All around the world, Biblical events are playing out. We have experienced major floods, earthquakes, fires and tornadoes. There have been swarms of locusts devouring land. I read somewhere that a river literally had turned red. I even saw a picture of a seven-headed snake found on a public road. These signs and events were previously documented in our Scriptures. For whatever reason, these same signs seem to be repeating themselves today.

We are living during Biblical times. Lucifer got caught in the true light, and the actions of his demons are being exposed. The Great Awakening is upon us and disturbing acts of evil are being exposed. Brace yourself! The false light of Lucifer will soon be revealed along with acts of evil more shocking than you may realize.

Belief is a powerful magic. It has been written that faith alone can move mountains. If my pen is my sword, then He has armed me for this apocalypse. Our judicial system has been turned into a weapon to be used for the advantage of the wealthy. My only move is to legally fight back with words that may protect me from the corruption of our judicial process. If I can be tortured in plain sight, imagine the pain they could inflict on me if I am locked in a cell or padded room.

Since the beginning of man, we have searched for a purpose. We have searched for a creator to worship. Humankind has worshiped stars, planets, animals and God. This worship has included many false gods and prophets as well. Some cultures believed the world was being carried on the back of a giant turtle. Some cultures today still worship cows. I call this maze of beliefs the Devil's persuasion, and it is his most powerful influence over us.

The entire point of humanity, I believe, was to have us believe in ourselves. It makes no difference what you choose to worship. We are created in His image. Free will is our true creator. We all have His power, and we are living now in the Kingdom of Heaven.

Why do you think Lucifer is trying to create Hell on Earth? Lucifer is resentful that we were given his power. Using persuasive influence and powerful weapons of witchcraft and evil, we humans are relinquishing more and more of our God-given power. We are close to being enslaved and our free will is eroding. God isn't going to come down and save the world. He gave us His power so we can save ourselves. He works through us, not for us. Therefore, angels around the world are waking up.

It makes no difference what you choose to believe or worship. You could pick up the first stone you see and pray to it every night. If you chose to be good and contribute to harmony, the stone could represent goodness. Your actions define you.

If you don't like who you are, then change what you do. Every person knows the difference between right and wrong. No matter what you choose to worship, if your actions are good, then you are on the right path.

If you chose to do evil while possessing the free will to know the difference between right and wrong, then you will find yourself on the wrong path. Most of you are on the wrong path because of the Devil's persuasion. The seven sins are the ammunition for this weapon. If more and more people choose to do evil, Lucifer will win and his vision of Hell on Earth will be realized.

Consider the word "good." If you lose one of the 'O's, you are left with God. Sometimes, doing the right thing means making a sacrifice. If the heroic attorney didn't sacrifice his own safety or take the chance of having his own reputation destroyed, Epstein would still be trafficking millions of underage children. This attorney could have taken the bribe or allowed the fear from the many death threats inhibit his effort. Instead, he sacrificed himself and his career because he knew the difference between right and wrong. He sacrificed the "O" and found God.

Now look at the word Evil. If you add a "D", you get Devil. Anytime you are compensated to act against the free will of God, you are faced with the Devil's influence. This is how the Illuminati has been buying souls. The army of demons recruits souls by offering money, vacations, career advancements or favors in return for supporting his vision of Hell on Earth. If you find yourself accepting something in return for a devilish favor, you are adding that "D" to evil, which invites the Devil into your life.

You are hereby burdened with the task of discovering who you are and what path you choose. Will you help wake up the world so we can regain our free will to do Good? Or has our spirituality been vaccinated away already?

The combination of Daniel's life, my connection to it and our perceptions of the current world are colliding. Daniel has been experiencing paranormal events his entire life. I believe my spiritual brother has control over this awareness and can project himself into peoples' lives as I have recently learned to do. He may have even willed a cancerous tumor to shrink away, considering medical doctors have no alternative explanation. Daniel is special and I still need to discover the purpose behind his frequent paranormal encounters.

How can Daniel help me? Do these stories and the thoughts I am ascribing hold a hidden communication? The only way to find answers is to keep going.

Dream Walking

Daniel may have paranormal demons trying to prevent his true power from being acknowledged. On the other hand, I have human demons trying to get me to kill myself or someone else. The more Daniel and I proceed with our sessions, the more I am attacked. The induced pain makes it difficult for me to do much of anything. The energy we created with this session has led us down a dreamy gauntlet.

A few events occurred in the last few days that could solidify my belief that I have opened some new doors to the paranormal world. Lori is the woman who I am currently living with. She continues to support me regardless of the physical and emotional trauma. But Lori has been hearing strange noises in the apartment while I am not home. The other day, she saw her closet door open on its own. I am not sure why she is now witnessing paranormal events or seeing shadow entities. Maybe because I am in Daniel's life, these entities are trying to get to me.

The other day, Daniel and I were on the couch in his basement. My peripheral vision caught a shadowy figure peeking around the corner at the top of the stairs. I looked at Daniel and he said, "Don't mind him. He's just curious about what we're doing."

The sight of this figure didn't scare me, but rather made me more curious. The way Daniel nonchalantly told me to ignore the figure proves he has been desensitized to these entities. They have become a part of his daily life. I am sure the more we continue with our journey, the more unexplained phenomena we will encounter.

To the best of my knowledge, we have a few different levels of sleep, or of consciousness. With each level of sleep, one dreams more vividly. Some psychology books claim that to dream you must be at the REM (Rapid Eye Movement) level. I disagree. I believe a person can dream while fully awake and preoccupied. Some call this phenomenon "daydreaming".

So, what is a dream? I claim that dreams are electrical impulses that carry data to the brain. Even though people are unconscious during sleep, their brains are active. Perhaps an event during life or a movie previously viewed contributes to a person's memories while unconscious. Daniel claimed he learned how to box during his dreams. He was watching a lot of Bruce Lee movies at the time, which may have contributed to these instructional recollections. I personally had dreams which were movie-like and entertaining. In my last book, I embarrassed myself and wrote about a recurring dream I had when I was a young boy. This recurring dream may have been a foreshadowing of how I am being crucified today, thirty-five years later.

I never gave much thought to my dreams, which demotes them to coincidental nonsense. The question I hope to answer is this: "Do our dreams hold a deeper meaning, or are they simply coincidental nonsense?"

I have read that certain dreams can be analyzed to give people direction in their lives. I've been told it is rare to have dreams about flying. I've had several dreams in which I was able to fly. So, what does this mean? Psychologists say that certain colors hold meaning. One of them wrote that if you see blood in your dreams you should expect to have a tragedy in your life. Some people dream of drowning or falling. Depending what is going on in their lives, these dreams may provide answers or guidance. If this is true, though, who is providing the guidance?

If my claim is right about dreams being electrical impulses sent to the brain, then a person can dream at any point, not just while sleeping. Sometimes I catch myself drifting away into a particular thought. Have you ever taken a drive and after you've arrived at your destination, you felt a little odd because you didn't remember the entire trip? In instances like this, our brain goes into auto pilot and your mind drifts into another reality. Sometimes, a person is so absorbed by a day dream, they miss their stop on the bus or train. Sometimes people forget they have a roast in the oven. The day dream may become so deep, it may take a violent shout from another person to snap the dreamer out of a particular trance. Therefore, I do not believe one must be asleep to experience this magic of the mind.

I have witnessed people get induced into hypnosis. The subject is awake; however, they are no longer in the same reality while under the spell. The hypnotist is controlling the subject's dreams. If another person can manipulate a person's dream, then I believe a person can learn how to control their own dreams as well. Some refer to this method as Lucid Dreaming. Have you ever heard of a Dream Walker?

To dream walk is to walk or transport one's consciousnesses to observe and heal the patterns and events transpiring in many alternate realities and time lines. Dream walking is to see the nature of the structure of what created them and to partner with God to find and remove reality boxes, or dark portals used as Consciousness Traps. I know it sounds heavy, but much like anything in life, the more you practice, the better you become.

Most people chalk up dreams to coincidental nonsense. Believe it or not, many people have dreams about certain events only to have those events come to reality sometime later. For example, Lori had several dreams in which came to fruition after the dream occurred. Perhaps her sixth sense is the reason we have connected so well, despite the ten-year gap in our age. She once dreamed she received an awakening phone call from her Uncle Denis, explaining her Grandfather had passed away. It was an emotional dream, but like most people, Lori chalked it up to coincidental nonsense. A few months later, Lori was woken up by a phone call from Uncle Denis, who explained her Grandfather had committed suicide.

Part of my responsibility as a scribe is to find meaning or purpose. This was horrifically saddening news for Lori, but what made it more difficult was recalling the dream she had a few months prior. Her Grandfather demonstrated no signs of wanting to harm himself. One day, he just decided life was too difficult to bear. Was the dream Lori had months before a sign something was wrong with her Grandfather? Was this a spirit, a ghost, or something paranormal trying to get Lori to prevent the suicide of her Grandfather?

I believe we all get communication from other worldly entities. After all, this entire project is meant to expose these many forms of communication all around us. I imagine most of us are too socially conditioned to acknowledge these subtle messages. We all get influence from a magic not of this world, whether it is through another person, a situation, a spirit, or even a dream. My question remains; Why are we not listening?

I suppose part of the issue with recognizing subtle forms of paranormal communication is they come in fragments. I suppose it may be difficult for some entities to make physical contact in our realm. I have heard many paranormal investigators make the claim how a spirit may have a difficult time breaking through the vale. Some ghosts can make a knocking sound or even move a chair across the room. Obviously, some forms of the supernatural are far more capable of making themselves known to us. A few of these examples would be possession, poltergeists, shadow figures, and even the UFO's we see flying in our skies.

When I was deathly ill from a mold infested house, my first experience with automatic writing provided my family a sign. I wrote a poem about God and the Devil called, "Ignorant disbelief". I was explaining how fungus allowed the Devil into our lives. My narcissistic mafia father-in-law used it against me and told the FBI that I was mentally unstable. That poem is now locked away with my accounts and are still under federal investigation for unknown reasons. If my family would have really read that poem and listened to the subtle message, they might have understood my illness. Only now do I realize mold is more Biblical than anyone could have ever imagined. Remember, it was not a forbidden apple which allowed evil into the garden. It was a mushroom.

If Lori would have taken her dream more seriously, maybe she would have tried to speak with her grandfather more, and perhaps, gave him a reason to live. So how many of us get some form of subtle communication everyday but choose to ignore the message? How many of these messages are given to us during our dreams?

What makes this concept of dreaming so enchanting is that our minds are active without us being in control. I am infatuated when I learn of stories proving the mind is still active after someone is clinically dead. There have been many documented cases where a person has flat lined, however, once they are brought back to life, they can recall and describe dreams. How can the mind still dream even with no electrical impulses being sent to the brain?

I understand how the body can still twitch and move even after the heart has stopped beating, so obviously the body still holds some energy soon after death. If you ever saw the movie Weekend at Bernie's, they made a hilarious joke about this concept when his mistress came to visit. Not knowing he was already dead, she apparently was able to find some remaining energy. All joking aside, the recollection of memories after one is declared dead is mystifying. Magic of the universe needs to be acknowledged so we can prepare ourselves against the Devil's persuasion. Our mind is the true garden, created with free will to do good. If we get tricked into doing evil, we contribute to Hell on Earth. We must be able to know the difference.

Daniel was still dreaming about the lives of the people around his daily routines. He wasn't dreaming about individuals he knew well, though somehow he was getting accurate information about random people. Daniel has become a little addicted to the feeling of fasting and continues to experiment with this type of cleansing. One day, about a week left in a particular fasting, he had a dream which led to an out of body experience.

He was awoken by the alarm clock and asked for ten more minutes as he hit the snooze button. Please recall that some areas of study state dreams are induced only in the REM stage of sleep. Daniel was just awoken by the alarm, so whatever sleep he briefly fell back into was probably not REM (Rapid Eye Movement) sleep.

During this ten-minute snooze, Daniel had a dream about fighting demons. I could tell by his emotions that the dream he experienced was vivid. He described being attacked by several demons, much like how zombies attack people in shows or movies. These entities were swarming him from every angle.

When Daniel grabbed these demons to fight back, they turned to water. With just his touch, these demons liquefied, and the water dropped to the ground with a splash. Even more curiously, Daniel described people in his dream who were possessed, as well as the actual demons. When he went to touch these possessed people, water began pouring out of their necks, much like the gills of a swamp monster. When he laid his hand upon them, the demons inside poured out, cleansing the person of the demon inside.

While in a staircase of a building, these demons and possessed people were coming at him from every direction. Daniel raced up the stairs to get to the rooftop. As he opened the door from the stairway onto the roof, he saw a dark entity with large black wings, much like the wings of a crow. Somehow, he knew this demon was controlling the hive and was the main entity responsible for the swarming attack. Daniel has met his match.

As Daniel went to grab this entity, the demon's large black wings began to flutter. Daniel tried to hold on but the power of this being was too strong. Daniel lost his grip and the Demon freed itself, hovering just above his reach. Then, as the Demon was fluttering slightly above Daniel, the entity swooped in to attack. This demon engulfed Daniel with his dark wings and outreached claws. After a bit of a struggle, the monster tried to bite his neck, much like a vampire.

Daniel dropped to the ground and rolled up into the fetal position, like a human canon ball. He said to himself, "I need to get back." "I need to return to my physical body which everyone knows", he proclaimed to himself. Suddenly, Daniel opened his eyes. For a split second, while laying paralyzed on the bed, Daniel saw a light rushing towards him. He describes this phenomenon as his spiritual self-crashing back into his body. As this force reentered his body while lying still on the bed, the impact was so fierce it nearly knocked him off the bed and onto the floor.

I will dive into some of my thoughts and analysis in a bit, however, the physical force which Daniel explains stimulates my curiosity. When he explained how his spiritual, dreaming self-reentered his true self, Daniel described an unexplained force which hit him like a ton of bricks.

For whatever reason, I can remember every detail and line from movies or shows. I can name several movies where this concept is mocked. In the comedy sequel Ace Ventura, the character of Jim Carey describes this exact scenario. While meditating and seeking answers, Ace had an out of body experience. As the scene comes to an end, his spiritual self flies back down into his real body and knocks him over. The scene was funny and made us all laugh, however, I have stated several times before, "fiction is fact."

This phenomenon made me do a little digging and I discovered hundreds of stories which explain the same type of shock or force when people explain their own out of body experiences. I am not just talking about scenes in movies, though real-life stories. With the help of either a witch or an Angel, I too had an out of body experience which was described in my last book during the Ramble of Magical. I did not, however, experience the force of having my dreaming self-enter my real self. Based on Daniel's description, the countless other stories I stumbled upon, and the fact fictional entertainment mocks this concept, I believe the force caused from the spirit reentering reality is more common than I originally perceived. This entire concept got more credible with a testimony from Daniel's father.

A short time after this experience, Daniel began to explain his dream to his dad. Before he could even finish the story, his dad said, "Stop." Daniel replied, "what do you mean stop?" His father went on to share a story about a woman he once knew. She told him a similar story regarding a dream and described the same force encountered from the spirit self-reentering the physical self.

"So, what are you saying?", Daniel asked his father. Daniel's father explained, "I thought this woman was just bat shit crazy for a long time, but now that my son has experienced the same situation, I believe it to be true." The sad irony of it all is this poor woman spent her entire life being ridiculed for explaining the magic she witnesses throughout her life. We all receive it to some degree, but at the same time we are programmed to ignore.

The more I think about dreaming, the more I become confused. What separates a dream from just a thought? If we close our eyes and pray to a higher power, are we dreaming? When we meditate, exercise, or drive a car while our minds drift away, are we dreaming even though we are wide awake, in auto pilot? If we can get answers or predictions of future events through our dreams, can we get the same type of guidance while our minds are in "day dream" mode?

Perhaps a dream is a type of out of body experience. When we wake up, many people don't give a second thought to the dream they might remember. The lack of thought moves the dream off their memory map and soon is forgotten. Maybe every dream is a form of communication. Social conditioning has worked so well, people are so preoccupied with daily life, we miss subtle messages. I believe our world is in the process of being conquered by a Luciferian Force, known as the Illuminati. We are not listening to the guidance, even when the guidance comes from another galaxy, like the 1977 communication from the voice of Vrillon. We didn't listen to George Washington warn us how the Illuminati has infiltrated the Free Masons and they have a bad intent for the new World.

Daniel was working at a restaurant inside the casino. The entrance of this upscale delicatessen leads out to the casino floor where a row of slot machines lined the front of the restaurant. The irony of this story is how soon, thousands of my own footsteps would be implanted over that same location. Cameras watched my every move, and I was quite good supervising the floor. If there is any weight to the theory of Last Thursdaism, then the video surveillance of both Daniel and I could hold more value to my own perceptions. In this theory, universes are created from our digital fingerprint, creating infinite number of our own realities. This concept is an entire study; however, the idea should at least be acknowledged.

Daniel was standing by the host's stand one day and witnessed a woman collapse. She was sitting at one of the slot machines right out front and just fell over onto the casino floor. Daniel is the type of person who wants to help, knows he can help, but always seeks guidance first. Daniel prayed to himself as the woman was crunched over on the floor, "Should I lay my hands on her and pray?" Daniel heard a deep voice reply, "No, it is Jerry's turn."

Daniel looked around; however, it was clear he was the only one who heard this voice. His coworker Jerry came up to the stand to see what was happening. Jerry said to Daniel, "my hands feel like they are on fire." "I have this urge to put my hands on her," Jerry added. Daniel told her, "go over and put your hands on her." Jerry looked at Daniel with a little confusion, but something prompted her to walk over to see if the woman was alright. Now it turns out, the woman was a recent guest in the restaurant. She sat at a table and ordered Mazza Ball Soup. Jerry recognized her right away which added more empathy towards the situation.

As Jerry bent down and placed her hand on the woman's shoulder, Daniel noticed the computers and printers went on the fritz. Receipts printed and were spitting out of the printer like the machine was possessed. All the lights in the restaurant began to flicker. Daniel grabbed one of the receipts, just for his own curiosity.

The paramedics came and the women was carried away with nothing catastrophic, however, the event became more paranormal when Jerry walked back into the restaurant. Daniel was standing at the podium, holding evidence to his other worldly acknowledgement. He handed Jerry one of the receipts retrieved from the dozens produced. When Jerry looked at the slip, her face turned white with disbelief. The ticket had the woman's table number on it with her order of Mazza Ball Soup from earlier that day. When they checked the dozens of other receipts piled up from the printer to the floor, Daniel and Jerry were shocked to see each receipt read Mazza Ball Soup. Some forms of communication are subtle, though some just scream for recognition.

Perhaps the situation provoked some additional conversation between Jerry and Daniel. She began to confide how she has always wanted to learn about the powers of natural healing. I don't know if Jerry's touch helped the woman or not, however, something strange happened regardless. The voice Daniel heard, providing direction to send Jerry to the woman in his place, as well as the computers going biz-irk, leads me to believe some form of other worldly communication was received. Jerry even mentioned to Daniel how her hands felt like they were on fire. She had a strange urge to help, but for what purpose though? Many people ignore these kinds of events and forget they even happen. What is the purpose of me writing about these messages now?

When Daniel prayed for direction, maybe he was day dreaming. Maybe the entire point was to awaken a power inside of Jerry so she will pursue a certain path of knowledge. Perhaps there is someone in Jerry's life who needs her to be strong. If Lori would have acknowledged the dream about her Grandfather, maybe she could have helped him cope with his demons.

If I would have analyzed my reoccurring dream as a child, perhaps my attention to the dreams could have prevented me from being set up and accused of some awful woman's rights violation. I am literally being executed by governing powers. We receive subtle forms of communication every day in magical ways. These messages come during dreams, prayers, life situations, and during everyday encounters. These clues can be interpreted with infinite explanations or outright ignored. Perhaps part of the purpose of this journey is to get people to start listening.

Think about your life alone and consider any troubles or tragedies you may have experienced. Were there any signs prior to the situation? Can you consider anything at all which might have been communication, warning you of a future problem or tragedy?

A few weeks past and Daniel was still experimenting with various forms of fasting. He was getting lonely in his life and it has been quite some time now that he was in a steady relationship. Daniel prayed to have a woman of faith come into his life. He sought for a willing, compatible companion to show him more love than he has ever received before. A true romantic. Daniel was looking for his puzzle piece to complete his current picture.

One day Daniel decided to call Stephanie and travel out to visit. Perhaps it was his increasing loneliness which made him forget about the troubles in their relationship. I wrote earlier about our pictures changing throughout life. When you try to keep the wrong puzzle piece in a particular spot, it will distort the overall picture.

Stephanie was very welcoming. Considering they spent nearly a decade together, a certain level of emotional equity created a love between them both. One night during the visit, Daniel and Stephanie were sleeping on the bed. Once again, Daniel had an out of body experience. He stood over the bed looking at himself and Stephanie sleeping.

As Daniel looked up, he noticed a figure standing in the doorway, though nothing dark or threatening. He couldn't make out any character details and described the figure as a shadow. He could tell this figure was a woman and even though his view was dark, he saw a glow from this shadow. Then, he heard a familiar voice. A voice which could never be forgotten. It was the same tone and fierce verbosity he heard as a young man when his name was called out, three times.

The voice exclaimed, "If you get back with this woman, you will surely lose that woman." When Daniel woke up the next morning, he felt confused. This was a very lonely time for Daniel, and he was searching for companionship to give him purpose. Reconnecting with Stephanie was an attempt to fill that void, but Daniel knew both of their jig saw puzzles had changed. He parted ways with Stephanie and returned home.

For the next few months, Daniel became numb. He started to live through his daily routines as if he were on auto pilot. Daniel went to school and work and was coasting through the days without any true direction or purpose. He began to feel lost and the way I imagine this period of Daniel's life was one long day dream.

One day while working at the casino, he laid his eyes upon a new employee named Paula for the first time. Daniel saw Paula from afar, but no matter the distance, his gaze beamed like he was looking through binoculars. Everything else around him became blurred and Paula was glowing with specific detail from across the casino floor. With an unwavering confidence, Daniel walked right up to this enchanting sight of a woman and introduce himself. He boldly spoke, "my name is Daniel Collazo, everyone calls me Rocky." Paula was taken off guard by the sudden introduction and responded with the question, "What?" as she gave a puzzled look back toward Daniel.

He repeated himself and said his name was Daniel, this time reaching out his hand. When she placed her soft hand into his, Daniel felt a warm, peaceful sensation rush over him. For a moment, he described the feeling of being on a tropical paradise with not a single concern to weigh him down. I wrote before how it may take a shout from another person to wake someone out of a day dream. Daniel was coasting through the daily routines, almost like acting out one long day dream. Paula's introduction into Daniel's life may have awoken him from auto pilot.

As Daniel came out of a euphoric trance, he found himself still shaking Paula's hand. The overwhelming feeling he got from this woman freaked him out a bit. Daniel walked into the kitchen area and asked himself, "was this her." "Was Paula the woman standing in the doorway back at Stephanie's," he pondered. Suddenly, Daniel heard a voice abruptly, and without doubt, proclaim, "No!" Daniel was alone and yet again he was faced with another worldly communication.

Daniel became more experienced throughout his life listening to these voices and allowing subtle forms of communication to guide his path. He did not, however, listen this time. Over the next phase of this journey, Paula and Daniel would begin to kindle a relationship. I am stuck on this concept and whatever force is flowing through my fingers will not allow me to move on. I mentioned how communication can come from both good and evil. Daniel received a magical feeling when he met Paula. Many times already, he has heard a voice. This time, the message he received saying "No", Paula was not the shadow of the woman he met in his dreams. Was Paula a false light? Was this another worldly attempt to prevent Daniel from meeting the woman he was meant to find?

One day while bored at work, Daniel was standing off to the side swinging his hands, clapping to a rhythm in his head. Paula intentionally walked by Daniel as she too was drawn into this companionship. She tried to think of something to say to show Daniel she was interested in getting to know him better. As Daniel was swinging his arms, Paula told him that he could clap loudly. A silly thing to say, but I can remember a time when girls did some peculiar things to get a boy's attention.

Daniel replied, "you should hear me clap in church." Daniel wanted her to know right away he was a man of faith. Maybe he was testing her reaction because he couldn't get the voice out of his head. As the reader, I would like you to try and understand how difficult it is for a person to experience the multitude of paranormal activity Daniel has witnessed so far throughout his life. I am only including a few examples since my publisher thinks I may ramble a bit. Daniel was questioning why he was so drawn to Paula, despite his guiding voice telling him, "No." Then, Paula replied to Daniel's comment regarding church and said, "Let me guess, he talks to you too."

Her comment shook Daniel to his core. Not many people realize Daniel constantly sees and hears things, not of this world. To have a girl he is so drawn to make a statement insinuating such an understanding provided him a spiritual light. Again, I find myself pondering, "was this a false light?"

About a week later, Daniel had another dream. At this point in our journey, I am convinced Daniel is tapping into some unacknowledged abilities to dream walk. He began dreaming he was standing on a street where large brick town homes lined the road on either side. He noticed an older couple walking on the sidewalk, approaching one of the houses. He figured something must be significant with this street. He saw the old couple approach the door to a house, however, their faces were distorted. They entered the house and disappeared inside to the left. Daniel then saw Paula walking down the sidewalk and approaching the same house. Daniel walked over to greet her and pleaded with Paula to wait. "Let me check it out before you go in the house," Daniel told her.

Daniel noticed to the left of the entrance where the older couple vanished inside the house was nothing more than a wall. So where did this distorted couple vanish to when they walked inside? "Were these people ghosts?" Daniel pondered.

He began to climb the staircase to search the house. As he got to the top of the stairwell, he noticed several cats. These felines walked over to Daniel and without fear, began to paw and rub against his legs. Daniel felt a sense of being adored by these cats. From the ones pawing at his feet, he noticed one more so than the rest. This white cat seemed to be important somehow. When Daniel looked to his left down the hall, he noticed another cat sitting by the kitchen who wanted nothing to do with Daniel. A stubborn nonconformist if you will. He also noticed the couple who entered the house before Paula were nowhere to be found.

When Daniel woke up, he obsessed over the details of this lucid dream. He figured Paula must have lived on that street and probably in that house. He knew the cats he saw held meaning but couldn't grasp the significance of this older couple who disappeared into the house. He desperately wanted to seek more of an understanding and eagerly awaited a chance to question Paula later that day.

While they were at work, Daniel took the opportunity to pry into Paula's personal life in hopes of finding some purpose to his dream. He advised Paula how he takes the bus to and from work and school. He confirmed with Paula how he doesn't drive, so there was no way he could have been stalking her. He was trying to control her reaction from hearing about this dream. I am sure Daniel is used to people freaking out about his abilities. Do you remember the teacher who read the note Daniel wrote in class predicting the lights were going to turn on by themselves? The teacher said, "Stop it, you're freaking me out." Daniel has naturally developed a way of asking questions without scaring people away.

The house which Daniel described in his dream was soon confirmed by Paula to be the same house her and her husband were recently looking to move into. The white cat matches the description of the pet cat Paula had as a child. The stubborn cat who ignored everyone in his dream seemed to fit the personality of her parent's pet cat now. Daniel still questioned to himself, "who were these people that disappeared through the wall?" Since this session seems to be steering itself towards finding purpose within our dreams, I must consider why he is dreaming about Paula, her childhood cat, and her parents' cat? Why did he see the house her and her husband were going to buy to start a new life together? Future events will provide some insight.

Somehow, Daniel is tapping into truths and realities of other people. Examples so far have shown his thoughts and dreams providing truths from past, present, and future events. This is the basic definition of dream walking.

About a week later while at work, the day seemed to be quite unusual. Restaurants can predict sales based on previous weeks and years; however, this day was more random with fluctuating business. During one downtime, he handed Paula a note. The note read, "Your husband is cheating on you. He has been cheating before your relationship, during, and even now." Paula was prompted to question Daniel about his predictions. Much like the many other examples so far, he really didn't have an answer, however, he knew these visions were not predictions. His thoughts were fact. Paula seemed skeptical yet fascinated by Daniel's abilities to see outside of his own world.

Paula told Daniel a story of her own and began to describe a time when she was living back in Portugal. "I had a dream, and I was given the name Daniel," she added. Paula even supported her claim by requesting he confirms the story with her mother, who was also told about the dream.

I have a feeling Daniel assumes my thoughts too, so I am hopeful he does not take offense to my interpretations. I do not believe Paula's story to be sincere. This deceit leads me to believe more about a false light surrounding Daniel. I have learned women demonstrate some odd behavior when their emotions get in the way. To tell a tale of a dream simply to find a connection with Daniel is not genuine behavior.

Daniel continued to try and warn Paula how her husband was cheating on her with a girl Maria. Instantly, Paula confirmed she knew a Maria. She was a dark-skinned girl who was cousins with her husband. Daniel told her, "Maria is not his cousin."

Paula was still skeptical, however, his concern for Paula's well being created an attraction. Paula began to offer rides to and from work and they became friends over a short period of time. One day while they were at work, Daniel told her, "Mark my words, your husband is hiding in the trunk of the car."

Paula thought he was kidding at first, though the seriousness of his tone began to instill concern. While they were approaching her car, she tried to get him to walk away, but Daniel refused. He didn't have anything other than a friendship with Paula at this point and Daniel is not one to hide.

Approaching the car, they could tell the back window was steamed over and once again, Daniel's intuition proved to be accurate. The car door opened, and they stood in place witnessing two legs pop out and stomp the pavement. Paula's husband crawled out from the back seat and began to stab a finger in Daniel's direction. Daniel has several boxing trophies and knocks out many of his opponents, so while capturing the scattered bits of detail I smirk to myself, eager to see if this guy gets knocked out.

"Is this Daniel", Paula's husband demanded to know. Paula tried to lie at first trying to keep Daniel's identity private. For what purpose, though? This is another subtle clue for me to ascribe for my own journey. There was nothing to hide at this point. They talked at work and Paula would offer Daniel rides. Paula demonstrated guilt. I believe it was not the guilt of the moment which poured out of her character, though the guilt from her entire life, past and future, which was oozing out.

Recall when Daniel had the dream of being attacked by demons and people who were possessed. When he touched these people, water would pour out of their necks and the person would be cleansed of the demon. I will hold off on my interpretations, however, I wanted to note this subtle message to leave more of an imprint in my own mind.

Daniel quickly acclaimed, "Yes, I'm Daniel." Paula's husband cowardly stood back, away from Daniel while continuing to jab his finger. He began trying to persuade Paula how Daniel was a drug addict. I find this accusation comical because I know the purity of fasting. Perhaps this was just another sign the jig saw puzzle Paula and her husband once shared has now changed. Daniel knew the type of man he was and whether it was magic, Angels, dream walking, or simply gifts we do not fully understand, Daniel knew Paula's husband was cheating with a girl named Maria. Their marriage was inevitably coming to a closing chapter.

They soon separated and began the process for a divorce. The failed marriage was difficult on the family. Her Parents had traditions downloaded into the fibers of culture while living back in Portugal. Her husband demonstrated many character flaws and sometimes these individuals fool people using narcissistic behavior and manipulation. Her parents put all the blame on their daughter and listened to the deceitful stories from her husband. Paula was "cast out" in a way and left to fend for herself.

Daniel took her in with open arms and invited Paula to stay with him at his apartment. They were still only friends at this point, but Daniel and Paula began to connect while living together for those next few months. Daniel soon forgot all about the voice which told him, "No", and was relieved he had found the companion he was asking for.

The divorce was finalized, and the news of Paula and Daniel was enough to begin gluing the family back together. They were invited over for dinner at Paula's parents' house. Shortly after they began to break bread, Paula's older sister who lived next door to her parents, barged into the dining room. She told Paula that she had to tell her something. In front of the table, she confirmed Paula's ex-husband was cheating on her with Maria, who was not a cousin. She went on to explain how Maria and her husband have been intimate before their marriage, during, and even now.

Paula broke down into to tears. She cried, "why couldn't I see this happening?" Daniel grabbed her hand and pulled her attention towards his words. Daniel spoke, "Because now, if you would have noticed it, you would have blamed God. But now, as you see it as I did, after I told you the truth, you will see God was just trying to save you from this marriage."

When I first captured these thoughts, I didn't feel the power of these words. It was only when I began my own version of dream walking where I felt the message. I am receiving a warming sensation coming over me even as I write these words. We have communication all around us, guiding us through our journeys. Most of us do not recognize this power talking to us through other people, events, and daily situations. Paula and Daniel began to build a picture of their own. Daniel was no longer lonely and seemed to have found genuine companionship.

I suppose the guilt of her ex-husband was eating away at his conscience. He knew was caught lying and wanted to seek closure. One day, He decided to call Paula and speak with them both. Paula's ex wanted to give his blessings. Daniel agreed to speak with him in the break area of work since the public surveillance would hinder any rash behavior. When the guy had the chance to speak, he turned his back to Paula and softly spoke towards Daniel. "Don't do this to me, I love her," he said.

Daniel responded, "No you don't. You don't know what love is. I love her." Since Paula was close by and the situation took an inappropriate turn, Daniel reached out his hand attempting to remove themselves from the conversation, the way a gentleman would behave. When Paula's ex-husband reached out and joined hands, time froze for Daniel. He was able to see into the soul of this man. A man who was indulging in sin, stealing from those around him. In that moment of shaking hands, Daniel somehow projected himself right into his mind.

What fascinates me about this entire compilation of stories, thoughts and rambles, is how I discovered abilities which I don't believe Daniel even realizes he practices. I am eager to study this real magic later in our journey. At this point, we still have some time to cover before our paths begin to collaborate. Just know while I attempt to illustrate this point on Daniel's timeline, I was stumbling through the ground floor of hell hurdling over the fiery traps of staged espionage. At the same time, however, I was also unknowingly listening to some guiding communication, or I wouldn't be around to write these words today.

As soon as Paula's ex-husband left, Daniel turned to Paula and warned her, "he has been stealing money from you and your parents all along." Although Paula did not think it was plausible, the guy managed all the family's money and certainly had the opportunity. Paula called the one bank, and sure enough, her account was drained.

A short time later while riding in the car with Paula and her mother, Daniel had an odd vision overwhelm his intuition. Daniel leaned forward and said to Paula's mother with an eerie confidence, "Mark my words. This guy has another account, and he will receive a balance of twenty-two thousand dollars which was stolen from your family."

Somehow, Daniel saw all of this in his head while silently sitting in the back seat. I discussed many ways in which a person can experience a dream. In my mind, I need to broaden the definition of a dream. Did Daniel pull some type of energy off Paula and her mother. The proximity in a car, the intimate conversation, and Daniel's focus on them both may have triggered another dream walk. I don't believe he understands what is happening or how he is deeply projecting himself into people's lives.

Paula tried to warn her parents, but her little proof and assumptions fell on def ears. The idea was even mocked a little by Paula's mother, but Daniel knew it was only a matter of time. Truth always seeps out eventually.

A few weeks later, mail was still coming to the house in her ex-husband's name. A bank statement appeared one day, and the curiosity overwhelmed the mother. She opened the statement and a profound humility swept over her face. It was a bank account statement with proof of transfers and deposits, all totaling twenty-two thousand dollars. How in the Lord's name did Daniel know every detail? Many of you may not have the ability to believe these stories. If you don't begin to believe, then I didn't do my job.

This was an interesting time for Daniel. He was getting pressure from outside forces which were manipulating how he wanted to live his life. Even Paula began to show nonverbal ques which made Daniel question the overall jigsaw puzzle. Daniel relied on public transportation for a while now. Paula's parents were pressuring them to get a car which created some unnecessary turmoil. Daniel did not feel the need to waste the money on a car at that time. "Be patient," he told Paula.

Daniel even began to feel trapped by the very apartment in which they were living in at the time. His father decided to move back to western Pennsylvania and Daniel stayed in the apartment along with most of the hand me down furniture. Daniel didn't feel like anything was his own. I recognize how Daniel wanted to create and gather his own life without anyone's help. When a man begins to get outside forces to dampen, even make this task impossible, it begins to eat away at the will of the man. True hero's and those who are empowered find a way to overcome all forces which may prevent the pursuit of fulfilling a conceived purpose.

Daniel decided to give the furniture back to his Dad. Paula and Daniel slept on the floor for a while and as the nights carried on, Paula began to show signs of displeasure. She began to jump the gun and act without discussing things with Daniel. For instance, she got a bed which caused a little turmoil due to the lack of communication and understanding. Daniel tried to get her to see the near future, as he did. He pointed around the empty, unfurnished room and told her how it is going to look once they built it together. Again, Daniel told her, "Be patient."

Daniel was influenced to drive back to western PA where he used to live with Stephanie. He had a storage unit with some of his own furniture and his own bed. Paula knew about Stephanie, but not vice verso. Daniel wanted to be completely open with Paula about his past knowing what she has already been through with the ex-husband. This made the short interaction a little uncomfortable, but Daniel picked up his belongings and drove back to his new life with Paula.

Perhaps it was the old energy which invited another supernatural event into Daniel's life. Maybe a negative aura from Paula invited this supernatural communication or the furniture itself was contaminated with something paranormal. Paula was about to witness some of the power Daniel possesses, especially relating to his dream walking.

Shortly after arranging the apartment, Paula woke up in the middle of the night by strange noises. She heard dresser drawers opening and shutting. She heard strange knocking noises across the room. She sat up in the bed and noticed Daniel was sound asleep. With a startled, soft voice she whispered, "Babe, do you hear that?"

While still sleeping, unknowing to what Paula was witnessing, Daniel unconsciously raised his arm into the air from a horizontal position. Within seconds of Daniel's hand rising, Paula testified the noises and odd phenomenon stopped. Daniel lowered his arm and continued to sleep. With no other disturbances, Paula eventually fell back asleep as well and discussed the events with Daniel the next morning. Daniel had no recollection to what occurred or what he had done.

For some reason, this session was difficult to push through. Whether the pain or distractions, I truly felt like I had a force preventing me from formulating my thoughts. I have thousands of people getting paid (devilish favors) by the Illuminati to attack me physically and mentally. This was the first time; however, I felt a paranormal force holding me down.

I could spend hundreds of pages expressing my thoughts and opinions on the concept of dreaming. If I were to focus on finding a single purpose for this entire session, I would like to consider the many different classifications of dreaming. One does not have to be asleep to dream. I need to ascribe how a great deal of enchanting communication is received during this magical trance of the mind, while awake or while sleeping. If we ignore the communication provided to all of us, then we will not acknowledge the Illuminati's plot to turn the entire human race into cattle. It is frightening, but true. The Elites of our world are drinking blood and eating children, fact not fiction. The problem which I see is the mass population is stuck in a fictitious dream world. I need you all to wake up now.

Doorways of Intuition

Working our way through these sessions, it has become clear to me that Daniel and I have been on a similar path our entire lives. Even before we were introduced to each other by the powers of the universe, we had been following a journey that would lead us to the same destination. Daniel has been confronted with paranormal entities his entire life. Throughout his life, he has been preparing for his own awakening.

On the other hand, I was traveling down a painful path to reach a similar level of awakening. All the persecution and torture inflicted on me is still happening today despite my squeaky-clean criminal record. If you read my previous two books, you will understand my own journey to this awakening. When a person begins to expose government secrets, they get heinously discredited to help protect those secrets.

While Daniel fights shadow entities, ghosts, and demons, I am seriously fighting real-life monsters. Daniel got to this realm using purification, fasting and meditation. I got to this point with an induced toxic poisoning. Today, we share the same insightful intuition. We both can use dreaming to see into other people's lives. Daniel is now able to witness the human monsters who surround me with a GPS-coordinated satellite terrorism program.

Daniel continued to accurately predict events. One night while he and Paula were in the apartment, they heard gunshots outside. The disturbance wasn't just a firecracker or a handgun—it was an automatic assault rifle. Allentown isn't the safe town it was when I grew up there. Daniel covered Paula with his body to protect her as they heard sirens. Through the window, they saw police cars and flashing lights.

The guy with the assault rifle came into Daniel's building and ran down the hallway. For a moment, it appeared the gunman had fled the scene, but Daniel somehow knew the shooter was going to come back down the hall. He considered telling the police outside that the intruder was in the building, but he didn't quite trust his instinct. Sure enough, within minutes the shooter raced back down the hallway toward their apartment. If Daniel had listened to his premonition, he would have asked the police to wait inside his apartment and they would have caught the guy.

The reason I am alive and working on my third book is because my intuition has reached superpower levels. I have begun to listen to the communications all around me. I have walked away from murder set-ups, drug traps and engineered attempts by the CIA to get me to hurt myself or someone else. There must be a reason for both of us to possess an enlightened intuition.

In the middle of that summer, Daniel and Paula were walking down a street in Allentown, my birthplace. Daniel was on the tail end of another lengthy fast. As they approached a church, Daniel stopped and asked Paula if she wanted to see something cool.

"This might be a little weird," he added.

Paula agreed and they entered the sanctuary. Inside, they sat in the back where about twenty other guests were sitting. A visiting minster from Puerto Rico was delivering a sermon. Just after the minster began, he paused and looked around the room, then He addressed the entire congregation and said, "Someone in this room is nearing the end of a forty-day fast."

Paula grabbed Daniel's arm and pulled. She couldn't believe her ears.

"Will that person please raise your hand," the minister said. "I want you to come with me."

Daniel did not raise his hand. Fasting is much more involved than just not eating food. Fasting means a complete sacrifice of body, mind and soul. This means purifying not only your body but adhering to promises and behaving in a pure manner as well. Daniel had made a promise to his Holy Father that he would not share what he was doing until the fast was finished.

The priest paused briefly, but since no one had confessed to fasting, he quickly moved onto his sermon.

How did the minister know Daniel was fasting? Even more intriguing, how did Daniel know something strange was going to happen in the church as they were walking by? Daniel had never met this minister before, and there is no logical explanation.

In my previous book, I defined magic as the absence of scientific rationale. Since I do not understand how this minister could have known someone was fasting, I must chalk this up to magic. Perhaps the minister was fasting himself and could somehow identify another person who was purified.

Do you remember the incident in which Daniel entered a classroom and felt a surge of negative energy coming from one girl? The priest had a similar type of intuition. Perhaps he knew it was Daniel but wanted to give him the opportunity to come forward on his own. Whatever the case, this is another example of how empowered individuals can feel, identify and listen to certain powers that cannot be seen or explained.

I have still not committed to fasting, yet I still seem to experience this type of magic every day   Being primed and brainwashed with engineered stimuli everyday as part of an organized stalking harassment, I have been able to open my mind to this power as well. By just looking at a person, I can tell exactly who they are and what they do. I can see situations happen before they take place. This magical capacity is surrounding all of us every day. A person's ability to witness these subtle messages depends on whether they acknowledge the communication. Unfortunately, most people overlook or ignore these sign, which are then erased from their own memories.

About a week after the church incident, while taking a break from fasting. Daniel walked back to that same church. When the sermon was over, he approached one of the priests and asked if the visiting minister from Puerto Rico was still in town. Daniel wanted to explain he was the one who was fasting. Unfortunately, the visiting minister had left. After hearing the story from Daniel, however, the priest asked why he hadn't raised his hand. Daniel explained that he didn't want to break the contract he had made with his higher power.

I am pondering what would have happened if Daniel had disclosed himself? Where would this visiting priest have taken Daniel? Was this a missed opportunity to become even more awake to the powers of the world?

Paula and Daniel both began to recognize subtle forms of communication from the universe. For a few weeks, Paula pointed out two white doves that seemed to be following Daniel around. No matter where they traveled, the two white doves were present. When they walked down the street, the doves were perched above them on a building or a lamp post. Even when they traveled, the doves seemed to be looking over Daniel. He explained to Paula that many animals may be Angels or Demons in disguise.

This relates to my own experiences. In my last book, during the "Ramble of Magic," I addressed this same type of intimacy with nature. I recently made friends with a squirrel I named Jerry. I have video of Jerry sitting in my hand, climbing up my arm and laying down next to me. Many times, while writing in the park, I would be accompanied by two white ducks. They would waddle up to my chair and sit with me. I started feeding them and soon these ducks became my friends. They would sit on my lap and eat from my hand.

I had many other birds give me the same type of affection. Even now I have a cardinal who follows me around and two turtle doves that watch over me when I travel. I have seen fish swimming around my legs and a large shark once greeted me in the ocean.

Daniel had squirrels waiting for him to come out of his apartment so they could follow him around. He began to connect with his new friends as I do. The way he explains his connection with wildlife is identical to my experiences. There must be a reason why we both are attracting romance with mother nature. I choose not to discuss my new profound connection with wildlife because I already have a hard time dealing with false perceptions of mental illness, but Daniel had Paula witness his experiences. She told me about how Daniel attracts wildlife. These subtle incidents are how the universe provides communication. The messages just need to be acknowledged.

One day, Daniel was waiting at the bus stop with a few other people. He didn't take notice of a man sitting behind him on the bench. As Daniel was standing there listening to music through his earphones, he heard a voice say, "Go talk to him." Daniel took off his earphones and looked around and again the voice spoke to him, but he failed to understand and pushed this incident out of his mind. Then the voice spoke to him even more firmly. "Go talk to him now!"

Daniel walked over to the man on the bench and said, "You're never too late." As Daniel told me this story, he seemed confused himself about the words he spoke and where they came from. He told me that the man looked up and predictably replied, "Excuse me?"

Daniel answered, "While you are still alone in this world, you can make the difference for yourself. He gives you the power to forgive yourself so you may be forgiven in his eyes."

The man started to fidget with disbelief and broke down in tears before looking up at Daniel. "How did you know?" the man asked.

Daniel replied, "I don't know how I knew, I was just told to come and talk with you."

A short time later, Daniel saw the man again, but this time the man wasn't held down by guilt. He seemed genuinely happy. Once the man saw Daniel, he walked up to him and said, "Thank you."

"Don't thank me," Daniel replied. "Thank our Father in Heaven because he loves you more than you think."

The man was grateful for Daniel's words and gave him a loving hug to show his appreciation.

This story fascinates me. Daniel has been hearing voices like this all his life. What perplexes me, though, are the actual words Daniel spoke. He may have heard the voice telling him to go talk to the guy, but where did Daniel get the words to speak? Prior to that day, Daniel didn't know who this guy was or what was going on in the man's life.

Daniel wasn't asleep, but perhaps he was drifting away in a daydream while waiting for the bus. I don't believe sleep is necessary to dream walk. Projecting yourself into another life or a different reality is done by pushing through some of those spiritual doors that are cleverly hidden and controlled. While a person with an active sixth sense is dreaming, his or her mind can initiate dream walking by chance alone.

Many distracting and controlling factors keep people from acknowledging the truth while awake. For instance, fluoride in our drinking water blocks the hidden abilities of our pineal glands. Social conditioning, debt, and technology keeps us too preoccupied to fully appreciate our human abilities. I hope people can start to acknowledge their pure power before conjoining their being with artificial life.

The voice Daniel heard was paranormal, but I am interested in the origination of the words he spoke. It almost seems that when Daniel opened his mouth to speak, someone else was doing the talking. I mentioned earlier how other worldly communication can come in many shapes, sizes, and forms. I believe much of my own writing is the result of this kind of communication. I believe Daniel has become a medium and was used to give this man a message.

Based on the positive attitude and gratitude of this man, the words Daniel spoke provided the guidance he needed at that time despite the fact Daniel had no idea what was going on in the man's life.

Daniel and Paula continued to build a life together, and Daniel was accepted into her family. One day, while they were visiting her parents, Daniel went upstairs to use the bathroom. While walking down the hallway to rejoin the family, something made him stop. As he glanced into her parents' bedroom, Daniel was overcome with a feeling that something was wrong. Negative energy was pouring out of the room. Eventually, he shook it off and walked downstairs, keeping the incident to himself.

About a day later, her parents discovered their wedding rings and other gold jewelry were missing from the bedroom. When Daniel heard the news, he instantly knew the items had been stolen and imagined the thief. Daniel somehow knew it was the boyfriend of Paula's older sister, Ana, who was living next door.

The situation became clear to Daniel. Paula's sister had known her boyfriend had stolen the earrings but had kept it secret from her parents. The boyfriend had disappeared soon after taking the jewelry. Possibly demons were trying to sabotage the current state of happiness by working through Paula's sister. Ana suggested to her parents that Daniel had taken the jewelry. It could be argued that Ana was trying to cover for her boyfriend, or even for her allowing a drug addict into their lives. Nevertheless, I believe a dark force was attempting to diminish Daniel's relationship, and therefore destroy his happiness.

Paula's mother called Daniel about the earrings. Daniel replied, "I am no thief. If no wrong were done to me, why would I do any harm to you?" The accusation stirred a fury inside him, mainly because his intuition had revealed the thief to him.

Angry, Daniel told Paula's mother, "Mark my words, when I see your daughter's boyfriend I'm going to put him in the hospital." Daniel knew he was a scapegoat and his anger may have created a power he did not fully acknowledge.

Let me share some of my insights about this. Our world is made up of energy. Everything in life creates a certain degree of power. This energy can be manufactured, like pushing a swing or rolling a ball into bowling pins. However, our thoughts, feelings and even group meditation create energy too. Even Daniel's own solo meditation previously had created enough energy to rid a home of a dark force, banished away shadow entities and possibly caused a cancerous tumor to shrink.

This energy has allowed Daniel and I to practice telekinesis. Though Daniel is far more advanced than I am, we can move a pin wheel using the energy from our minds, and Daniel can create ripples on the surface of water. He says you must demonstrate love and show respect for this energy to connect with telekinetic powers. This love and understanding allows our mind to join a force with an object like a pin wheel. I believe energy was created from the anger Daniel was experiencing after being wrongly accused of theft, creating a ripple effect in the universe.

After Daniel spoke those harsh words to Paula's mother, energy was channeled through his emotions. Amazingly, Ana's boyfriend went into the hospital the next day, though not by the hands of Daniel. To this day, the reason for the hospitalization is unknown. The entire episode reminded Daniel of a particular passage in the Bible" "Do not seek vengeance, for vengeance is mine."

I get attacked with both physical and psychological warfare twenty-four hours a day with the intention of making me lash out and harm myself or someone else. I am told by a higher power to forget about justice or revenge.

Dealing with the character assassinations that accompany COINTELPRO (also known as organized stalking), I have come to believe the truth will always rise. I haven't been able to speak to my daughter in years because I have been slandered as a pedophile, a tactic designed to make me to lash out and seek vengeance. Through writing, I found a way to hold onto a belief; the truth will someday rise through the scum.

Sometime later, on a random encounter, Paula ran into a friend and they started to catch up on their lives. She explained that her parents were upset with Daniel because they thought he had stolen some jewelry.

Paula's friend replied that she knew a guy who was doing drugs with her sister's boyfriend. "Maybe it was Ana's boyfriend. I know the two of them sometimes sold jewelry at a local pawn shop. I bet they used the money to support their habit."

To clinch the truth, neighbors of Paula's parents later mentioned that they had seen the boyfriend climbing out of the bedroom window before they knew the jewelry was missing. They thought the guy must have forgotten his key and didn't think too much about it. The evidence again proved Daniel's intuition to be correct.

The family tension began to subside since the evidence was adding up to clear Daniel. Perhaps from her own guilt, 'Ana soon moved into an apartment in Allentown not far from where Paula and Daniel lived. They all decided to simply let the past go and move on.

A short time later, 'Ana invited Daniel and Paula to her apartment for a visit. Daniel walked into the apartment and instantly felt a strange aura. He sat at the kitchen table and looked 'Ana in the eye. "Mark my words," he said again. "This place is haunted."

Daniel felt the presence of three spirits—a woman, a little girl and a man who exuded a dark energy. He tried to explain his feelings about these three spirits, but his warning went unacknowledged for a time.

Since 'Ana had moved nearby, they began to visit with her on a weekly basis. Over this time, strange incidents began to occur. 'Ana had two dogs that had recently given birth to a litter of puppies. She was upset because the dogs kept getting the bread off the shelf. Daniel heard the story but couldn't understand how the puppies were getting the loaf of bread since the shelf was well above their reach.

Daniel said to 'Ana, "Something is pushing the bread onto the floor." Daniel investigated where the bread was placed. He made sure the loaf of bread was flat, secure and high enough for the puppies to be unable to reach it. Daniel, alone in the kitchen, sat in the chair and tried to provoke this energy.

Suddenly, Daniel saw the loaf of bread being pushed off the shelf by an unseen force. He communicated what had happened to Paula and 'Ana. "I told you this was not the dogs getting the bread."

'Ana decided to put some cameras around the house. The family had a pet bird kept in a locked cage. While reviewing some of the footage, 'Ana became very unsettled when she saw the latch on the birdcage slide open on its own. The bird climbed out and perched on top of the cage. After a time, the bird climbed down and went back into the cage. To her amazement, she then saw the door close and the latch lock itself. The entire episode was caught on video and 'Ana shared it with Daniel and Paula. The way this paranormal event took place, it was almost like an unseen entity wanted to interact and play with the bird, though showed respect by closing the cage. Was this the ghost of the little girl that Daniel had sensed when first entering the apartment?

I try never to invest in a firm conclusion about things. Once you think you know something, your mind will automatically discredit any new information without even realizing the conditioned ignorance. If you consider this concept on a global scale, the governing forces have created a matrix. Everything the mass population believes is inaccurate.

> "When everything the American Public believes is false, the disinformation program will be complete."
>
> –William Casey, Director of CIA

Even though movies have been made about true events, people still formulate their own shallow perceptions about the paranormal. Numerous cable series are now popular sharing real life encounters with time travel, shadow entities, aliens, cryptids, and a plethora of supernatural encounters that cannot be explained. Even still, most people outright ignore these truths that surround us. Some of the forces are very dark and evil, which is why the world is beginning to see Hell on Earth. We need to learn how to identify these powers, both good and evil, to ensure we do not get fooled by a false light. If we do not begin to identify what is real, we will never be able to know the difference. Lucifer is clever.

Over time, visiting 'Ana and the kids became a weekly routine. A family unit began to form. And when a family comes together, secrets begin to be unveiled. Daniel began to witness many paranormal events through 'Ana and her family.

One night, 'Ana's son Brian woke up terrified. He stood up holding a trembling pet Chihuahua. Camera footage had captured Brian standing in the room looking at a chair. A shadowy figure of a little girl eerily occupied the chair looking back at Brian. He ran out of the room and closed the door, refusing to turn any lights off for the rest of the night.

'Ana showed the video to Daniel. When Brian came into the room the next morning, 'Ana's boyfriend Ernesto asked, "What were you doing up in the middle of the night?"

Daniel said, "Stop, you're telling him wrong." He turned to Brian. "You are not in trouble, Brian. When you got up, what happened? Why were you scared, looking at the chair?"

"I saw a kid sitting in the chair with hollowed out black eyes," Brian replied.

Hearing these stories or seeing them on television doesn't give you the full effect, which can only be realized by personal encounters and speaking with eyewitnesses. If you add personal experience to passion and will, worldly questions begin to create energy around the world. This energy has now created airtime on media for the sharing of intimate, true-life encounters. Universities have created research teams to study these phenomena and our own government outsources contracts to keep their heads above water with supernatural powers.

When Daniel walked into 'Ana's house for the first time and warned them it was haunted, he specifically described a man with dark energy, a woman, and a little girl. They kept that a secret from the children so as not to frighten them. One of the older siblings decided she wanted to research the history of the house. While going through microfilm and old newspapers at the library, she discovered that her address had been the scene of a gruesome event in which a man murdered a women and child there.

When she got back to share what she had learned, everyone was shocked except for Daniel who knew right away who was haunting the house. I did a little of my own research. The entire piece of land had been home to several witchcraft covens and individual activists before William Allen, founder of Allentown, came to town.

Over time, Ana started to believe she could control these entities and 'she began to think she had more power than she actually does. She told Daniel, "These entities are not bad." Daniel reminded her how she is not an ordained expert. He explained how she would have identified these spirits right away if she was truly in control. Daniel knows he is not fully in control either, so how could 'Ana be so arrogant?

I believe some of these past and current events which continue to affect 'Ana is a way for these powers to mock her. If you don't fully understand a certain power or concept, pretending to have the ability to control it creates a dark force and could allow negative energy into your life.

'Ana told me about a physical encounter in which she felt like she was being strangled. It seems 'Ana was not showing respect for the energy that was in the house and in return was physically attacked.

She explained that a while ago her boyfriend, Ernesto, had seen a woman's shadow on the wall. The light in the room made it impossible to accept a shadow could be present there. When everyone in the house was accounted for, he became very unsettled.

When 'Ana told Daniel about the incident, he warned, "Tell him to be careful." Somehow, Daniel had experienced a vision of Ernesto being pushed down the stairs and somehow knew Ernesto was going to blame it on the children. Daniel even explained this to Ernesto, warning him, "Don't blame the kids."

A few weeks later, 'Ana called Daniel with the news that Ernesto was in the hospital after being pushed down the stairs. "The kids must have pushed me," he grunted with disbelief.

I'm not dumbfounded by these stories anymore. But I am zeroed in on Daniel's specific powers. How does he know these things? Who are these guiding voices that tell him what will happen?

Remember how Nostradamus had predicted that two steel birds would take down financial towers? His vision, no matter how long ago it had occurred, didn't stop the plot from unfolding. Likewise, Daniel tried to warn 'Ana and Ernesto with his prediction, but most minds cannot comprehend the existence of such otherworldly energy. I believe trying to force a belief onto another person is the Devil's Persuasion. Even if we know the truth about something revolutionary like the two steel birds, the people who are aware of the prophecy cannot bypass years of social engineering so they fail to take heed. The level of willfully conditioned ignorance frustrates me to my core.

Everyone around Daniel's life seems to become a witness to his powers, myself included. Maybe Daniel is somehow attracting this energy. I have become drawn to these stories and share them using my own method of therapeutic release. Currently, my level of communication is amateurish at best, but I know I am being guided to write. Every time I experience the pain of my daughter's absence from my life, I write. Every time I feel electronic torture, I write. For what great purpose, though?

Session IX

Magnetic or Haunted

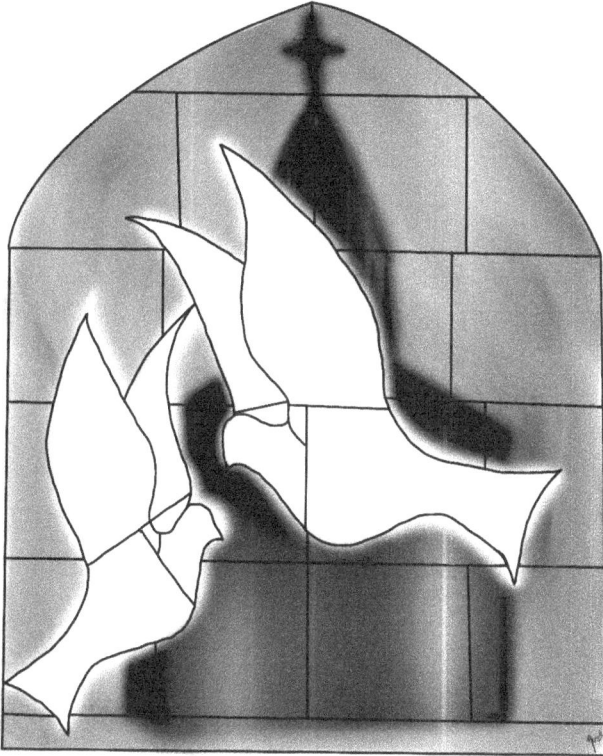

Daniel became a member of a cleaning team for the casino. Among his new work friends was a man named Manuel, his wife Maria and her cousin.

One day, while having a typical day at work, he entered one of the restaurants and walked by the dish area to begin cleaning. Suddenly, he noticed a shadow figure scurry away. He turned to find Maria's cousin belittling her about something. Quickly, her cousin left the area in the same direction as the shadow.

Maria's expression told Daniel that she had seen the shadow figure, so to confirm he asked, "Did you see it?"

"I saw a shadow move," Maria answered. Intuitively, he investigated her soul and replied, "It was a demon."

Maria explained that her cousin had been studying and practicing the dark side of witchcraft. It is not the area of study that makes something evil; the evil lies in the intent of the student. The devotion to any such craft may bring along unwanted entities. The energy projected while practicing rituals is a method of communicating, thus it's important to be careful who you are communicating with.

Since Daniel is constantly surrounded by otherworldly events, he tends to speak about them frequently as if they were everyday topics, like how I refer to my own targeting. Every day I get attacked with street theater. When I travel, enter a store or sit on my front porch, the Illuminati is staging my life like the Truman Show with everyday citizens so I don't even know what's real. These experiments also include sadistic, neural programming and induced pain.

I tend to refer to these incidents as normal everyday life, even though most people cannot fathom what it is like to be surrounded by an AI terror program composed of entire communities. For reasons still unknown to me, our government apparently allows the Illuminati to experiment, torture, and murder people based on lies and deception. I am a guy who is loved by many, has maintained a clean criminal record and who is working on my third book. Use your God-given free will to create your own perceptions of me and my life.

Daniel and a fellow co-worker was paired up to tackle the bar area in the convention center. This part of the casino is where all the major concerts and shows are held. Being the only two in this huge facility was intimidating. After some chit chat, it became clear the co-worker did not believe in anything paranormal. I know how difficult it must have been for Daniel to hold his tongue. I once heard the phrase, "Don't ever argue with stupid."

As they were cleaning up, Daniel and his co-worker heard footsteps in the distance—the sound of high heels echoing in the auditorium.

"That sound is coming from outside," the co-worker said.

After they both looked around the quiet concert hall, Daniel told him it was not, but he knew enough to limit his argument.

Suddenly, they both noticed a shadow. The dark figure portrayed an attractive woman wearing a long flowing dress.

The co-worker looked around the vast space for explanations. When he saw no possible source for the shadow, he turned back to glance at it one more time, but it quickly disappeared. While Daniel was desensitized to such phenomena, his co-worker was terrified and wanted to leave.

I wondered why the co-worker heard high heel footsteps followed by a woman's shadow right after arguing with Daniel about how he did not believe in the supernatural. Will he now become more awake?

The history of the casino may be relevant. The site was once the home of a renowned steel mill, Bethlehem Steel, which had experienced its share of tragedies. My grandfather used to tell me stories about how a man had fallen into a trench of molten iron. This was a dangerous profession, especially when workers were trying to keep up with the demands of WWII.

Looking back further than the history of Bethlehem Steel is also informative. I have spent many enchanting days and evenings writing at Monacacy Park in Bethlehem, Pennsylvania. There is a broken-down stone footing there of what used to be a house with an intact chimney. Off the main trail is an opening to a huge cave. The Moravians settled in Bethlehem sometime in the 1600s. When I write in this place, energy surrounds me. Our local news channel interviewed me while I was writing there on a warm winter's day.

The building in which Daniel and his co-worker were working speaks to me as well. The convention center creates enormous amounts of energy. You can probably recall being in a large crowd as everyone sang and celebrated the moment by swaying their arms or dancing to the same song. The combined group energy creates a euphoric sensation. After the show, you may have felt that the experience was awesome.

The pot you smoked and the beer you drank may have contributed to your euphoria, but much of that joy was produced from the crowd and not the music or the band. This is an example of the power of group meditation, for becoming one in the moment is a kind of meditation.

Now think about all the concerts and crowds held by this convention center in the recent past. This enormous amount of energy could have given power to some spirits of the past—at least generating enough energy to make them manifest. Perhaps it was Daniel alone who gave this shadow woman the energy to manifest in the room. More likely, it was the combination of both.

Moving along our timeline, I continue to explore my own version of dream walking. From projecting myself into Daniel's memories, I know the events he experiences come from various scenarios—not just a house or a large concert hall, but from wherever Daniel travels. I am understanding that he is not being followed by any energy, and neither am I. These events help me see there are energies all around us at all times. Daniel is just one of the few who can experience this other world that is colliding with our own.

Daniel eventually changed occupations. During life, it isn't just relationships that are a jigsaw puzzle that needs solving. Our professions, religions, families and personal needs are puzzles as well. For whatever reason, Daniel began working with a fire prevention company doing commercial jobs and industrial cleaning, which required some travel. For one job in upstate New York, he paired up with a woman named Amber. This was strictly platonic and work-related, perhaps because Amber was only interested in her same sex.

Daniel and Amber were sleeping in separate beds in the same hotel room near the work site when Daniel heard knocking on the sliding exterior door. He looked outside but saw no one there. Suddenly, while Amber remained asleep, Daniel heard a knocking sound from inside the room. The tapping seemed to come from Amber's bed board. This seemed like just another routine paranormal event for Daniel so he let Amber sleep through this paranormal activity. Perhaps Amber was having a dream that provoked the tapping.

The next day, Daniel told Amber about the events of the previous night. Amber explained that she was going through a traumatic time in her life. Her brother had recently died, quite tragically. The communication between Daniel and her motivated Amber to visit her brother's old room, possibly looking for closure. She stood in the center of his bedroom with watery eyes and called out, "Are you here?"

A tear was streaking down her cheek when she heard a BANG! No one else was in the room. Perhaps this communication gave Amber the closure she needed to move on.

I have presented many examples of Daniel encountering strange occurrences. As I continue to explore the dream world, I will add another episode. One night, while Daniel was out of town for a job, Paula and his son DJ called him on the phone. They frantically tried to explain that something was in the apartment. Their panic poured though the phone. They were hearing strange noises, they told him, and things were getting moved. Some items had vanished altogether. There was a threatening vibe in the apartment.

Daniel replied, "Put me on speaker and take me into the bathroom." As he explained this to me, I asked myself how he knew to go into the bathroom? Even DJ asked him that. "The bathroom is where most of these noises are coming from," DJ fearfully added.

Daniel spoke into the phone: "Be gone, you are not welcome here." These were the words he had used before to rebuke demons. Once he had learned how demons listened when he spoke, Daniel gained even more control over this unseen world.

Daniel was on the road quite a bit due to his job. While he was gone, Paula and DJ began to play with spirit boxes. They wanted to learn more about what they had just experienced.

A spirit box is probably my least favorite tool because the results can be interpreted in many ways. Basically, it is a gadget that randomly jumps from one radio frequency to the next allowing the spirit world to combine words from different radio and streaming outputs. Using wi-fi to operate a spirit box reinforces my skepticism. The old-time spirit boxes were built from those older tuning radios, which I find slightly more credible.

One time, while Daniel was away for a job, he woke up with an intense concern. He called Paula and his son to make sure everything was all right. Somehow, Daniel knew they were frightened.

"Yeah, everything is fine," Paula replied with a tone of uncertainty.

In the background, he heard DJ shout, "She just doesn't want you to worry!"

Now that a problem had surfaced, they began explaining to Daniel that strange noises were coming from the kitchen. The hairs on their bodies would stand up as odd electromagnetic chills overcame them. The overall atmosphere in the apartment was ominous. Paula and DJ sensed that they were not alone.

Once again, Daniel demanded that they put him on speakerphone. Then he addressed the entire apartment with anger: "You are not invited here, be gone. Leave my family alone!"

Whenever he spoke directly at an entity, the paranormal activity would subside. And every time Daniel would leave for another job, these entities perhaps thought it was safe to come back. When Daniel returned home from a job, he would smudge the apartment, blessing it with sage and prayer.

DJ once asked a spirit box if the entity feared his dad. The box instantly announced, "No." I have learned that demons lie, cheat and sin. It is in their character. Arrogance might have been the reason Lucifer was cast out of Heaven. These entities know Daniel can control them, yet they tried to instill fear in DJ by telling him they were not afraid of his dad.

The reason why I do not think all entities are afraid of Daniel, however, stems back to a dream. Somehow, I traveled to a place where I could see him fighting demons as if I were watching a movie. Although he was liquefying the demons he touched, Daniel met his match when he reached the top of a roof. A large, dark, winged demon was not scared of Daniel at all. Daniel prayed that he be allowed to return to his real body as this flying demon was trying to bite his neck. Daniel rolled up into a submissive ball to prevent the bite.

If I am right about dreams giving us communication, then I must conclude this dream is speaking to me.

Who was this dark flying Demon? Lucifer is an Angel who casts a false light over the Earth. I must consider the possibility that the entity that forced Daniel to retreat into his body could have been Lucifer. Was the power from the Dark Prince the reason Daniel felt such a strong force when he reentered his body?

The life we have experienced and the paths we have walked have led us to this moment in time. Our journey creates a message that goes beyond coincidental nonsense. I am fighting Lucifer in real time on this Earth.

Daniel may have seen Lucifer during his out-of-body experience. My name is Michael. When a person like Daniel makes a claim, I am a Nephilim and I am forced to listen. Corny as it may sound, Daniel and I both live in Bethlehem (Pennsylvania.) We are nearing the point where the past catches up to where we stand today. But as I time travel back and forth from past to present, I find it probable that neither Daniel nor I could defeat Lucifer on our own. Perhaps that is why we were brought together, to fulfill this biblical task.

Session X

No Time Like the Present

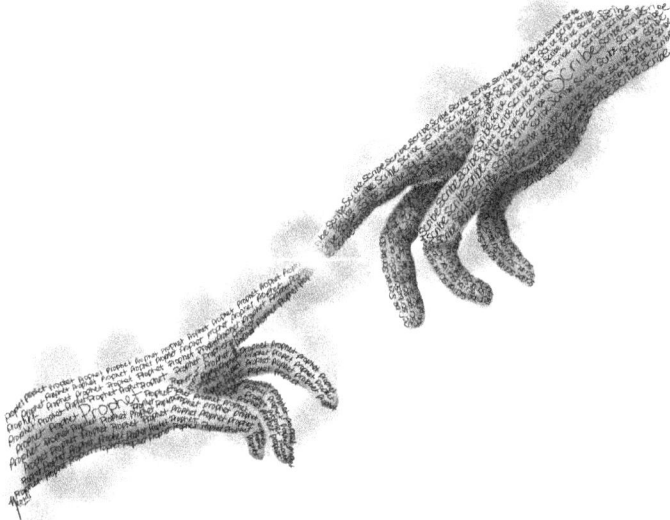

In this session, the past begins to collaborate with the present. I have been feeling an overwhelming weight that I do not know how to describe. Most of my pain is remotely induced, but I also feel a dark force clouding my mind and preventing me from writing. I was a bit intimidated before starting this session because I don't know how to mesh the past with the present. I had become accustomed to traveling down Daniel's memories and writing with my own version of dream walking.

As I continue to progress toward the current day, I will try to merge three concepts—our past, which led us here; the apocalyptic world of the current day; and hopefully some future direction leading to a purpose.

Daniel went to a family reunion in Dunkirk, NY. He learned that such an event can never live up to one's nostalgic memories.

While Daniel was attempting to honor his family traditions in 2014, my family was being intentionally torn apart. My targeting was well underway and the entire goal, as it still is, was to boost my suicidal or homicidal tendencies. Ironically, when I was working at the casino and overlapping Daniel's employment there by a few months.

My role as the Food and Beverage Supervisor for the casino was being sabotaged by women representing the Illuminati. This had also been done during my previous four jobs. When money and power want you dead, they use scapegoats to cover up intentions. In my situation, women were paid to lie and accuse me of some truly awful women's rights abuses. I can only speculate as to the reason. I will use Happy Place as a pseudonym for the forces behind these heinous attacks.

I now have thousands of demons (hired women) following a GPS, attacking me with psychological and physical warfare, and laughing at my pain. I was not kidding—I am at war with Lucifer and the empire he hides behind.

During Daniel's family reunion, he connected with his childhood friend, George. Before they became friends, George tried to start a fight with Daniel. He quickly learned Daniel isn't one to mess with. I enjoy looking at all his boxing trophies today, so I can imagine he was a tough little kid.

Their relationship grew into one like brothers. Their families were tight, and everyone knew each other well. George and Daniel both went to Bible study every week. Ever since that early altercation in childhood, they shared a brotherly bond.

Daniel decided to go visit George while he was in town for the reunion. George's entire family was happy to see him and they got to meet Paula. The little sister of the family, Brenda, was getting married the next day, so Daniel and Paula were invited to stay and go to the wedding. Before Brenda was engaged, she had told Daniel she would be blessed if he would be at her wedding one day, and then Daniel randomly, without warning, decided to visit at the time of her wedding. A wedding brings together family and creates an overall sense of happiness. Maybe Daniel was drawn to that family happiness and the visit wasn't random after all.

Daniel's family reunion took an interesting turn the day after the wedding when Daniel decided to go visit his aunt. He had learned that his Uncle Felix had been in the hospital for several months in a coma. With his Aunt Noelia and his cousin, Daniel and Paula drove to the hospital in Buffalo, New York, an hour away.

In the car, Paula asked Daniel, "Are you Ok?"

"I'm fine. Everything is going to be great," Daniel whispered back.

Daniel's words seemed odd to me—not the average response to that question in that situation. Somehow, Daniel knew it would all be fine.

At the hospital, only two visitors could visit at a time. Daniel patiently waited outside with the family until it was his turn. While waiting, though, , Daniel felt like he had to do something—he just didn't know what.

I recall many times when Daniel had just blindly acted, which in turn brought positive results. Perhaps while he sat in the waiting room he knew he was going to do something but had no idea what was to come.

The time came for Daniel to enter his uncle's hospital room with his cousin Jonny, a nickname for her real name, Janet Enoch. (When you grow up like family, everyone becomes a cousin.) They both kissed Uncle Felix on the forehead and Daniel bent down and spoke into his ear as his uncle lay there unconscious. "Tio, it's me, Daniel—Wilda's son," Daniel said. "I'm here.".

Daniel turned to his cousin and asked her if she wanted to pray. As they joined hands, they both felt a power come into the room. A gentle breeze tickled its way through the air, provoking goosebumps. They closed their eyes and Daniel led them in prayer. Once they said "Amen," both felt another surge of power fill the room. They said their final goodbyes, and as they began to leave, Daniel received a vision, or perhaps dream walked into his Uncle's mind. Daniel saw his uncle trying to get up. He turned back toward his Uncle and saw his legs twitching under the covers. Quickly, he walked to Uncle Felix's side and whispered, "Relax now, just rest."

When Daniel joined his family outside, he told his aunt and cousin, "Don't worry. He will be all right." Then with eerie confidence, he said, "He will be awake tomorrow." Daniel had no idea what made him say those bold words.

When they arrived back at the house, Daniel and his cousin, Jonny, wanted to know how Daniel was so certain Uncle Felix would wake up. Daniel told her the story about his classmate Zera who was the first person to call him a prophet.

Jonny suddenly said to Daniel, "Stop. I take it your mother never told you."

"Tell me what?" Daniel asked.

Jonny told Daniel that when Wilda was pregnant with him, Wilda decided to take a walk with Jonny down a road with an open patch of land. An old woman with black hair and a shawl appeared out of thin air, or so it seemed. This elderly woman pointed at Wilda's stomach and said with a cryptic voice, "What you have there is a prophet of the Lord." Jonny and Wilda turned and looked at each other, more out of confusion than anything else. When they turned back to the woman she was gone.

How could a woman disappear into thin air? Was she a mirage with a voice? How could this "coincidental nonsense" be overlooked for decades before it was finally mentioned again?

Jonny's story brought tears to Daniel's eyes. He felt a heavy responsibility and didn't know what to do with any of it.

"What could I do even if I knew?" he said to me later. The only thing Daniel seemed to fear was letting down his Holy Father.

As the scribe of this journey, I can proclaim with confidence, "Look at what Daniel has already done, with no true realization." I don't think Daniel understands he has been practicing his power all along.

The reason this story affected me so deeply is personal. Even as I write this sentence, I have Lucifer's demons harassing me, which is an immature attempt to break my mind. Daniel is the one who told me I was a Nephilim. If Daniel is truly a prophet of the Lord, then perhaps I should consider the idea that this entire project is a message. If our world ever needed to be saved, it is right now. Could this really be the direction of our journey? I am overwhelmed by the thought of such a biblical task, all while knowing I will still be crucified.

Moving onto the next set of events gave me more chills, as if someone were reaching inside me and trying to shake something loose.

Paula and Daniel were driving home after an eventful family reunion. Daniel hadn't planned on attending a wedding or making a trip to the hospital. About halfway back to Allentown the next day, Daniel sent a text to Jonny asking how Uncle Felix was doing.

Jonny texted back that Tio had woke up. Instead of providing any more details, Jonny demanded to know how Daniel had known Felix was going to come out of his coma. Daniel replied that he didn't really understand how he knew. He just did.

I suppose being a prophet is challenging since the role doesn't come with an instruction manual. Being a scribe is much easier. All I must do is write about what I see and learn while experimenting with some of the hidden magic around the world like dream walking.

But what if my role is more than just being a scribe? Like Daniel, I do not want to disappoint my Holy Father. If I am here to defeat Lucifer and save the world from a biblical holocaust, then where the hell is *my* instruction manual?

While Daniel and I were engaged in this session, we encountered (or perhaps provoked) an entity. I was lying on the couch with my feet hanging over the side. My back was supported by a bunch of pillows while I gathered pieces to the current jigsaw puzzle.

Suddenly, we heard a "BANG!" I thought it might have been from next door and didn't think twice about the sudden interruption. Daniel, however, got up to investigate. The neighbors were not home, and only Daniel and I were in our house.

When Daniel returned downstairs, he told me the noise had come from the glass shower door in the upstairs bathroom. Something had opened and closed it with enough force to get our attention. We had previously seen the heads of curious shadow figures peek around the corner with curiosity. I could argue the paranormal attention we are attracting is more communication which needs interpreting.

Within that same year, Daniel started to have some turmoil at work caused by a co-worker who was constantly making racist remarks, sleeping on the job and generally starting trouble whenever possible. Daniel's outspoken dignity must have rubbed this guy the wrong way because he began trying to make Daniel look bad at work. One day, to counter the co-worker's games, Daniel shot a video of him sleeping on the job and distributed it to the rest of his team. When the guy filed a complaint, Daniel's actions were grounds for termination.

This story was like what happened to me on various occasions. My job at the casino was being sabotaged too. Daniel's firing caused him to seek a new job, just as I often found myself doing. Daniel was soon hired at Big Foody's to perform various restaurant functions, but mostly deliveries. Much like every other job, Daniel's work ethic and unique character created strong bonds within his team.

Daniel felt a strange energy in the large building, which had been turned into a Bar and Restaurant. He couldn't quite put his finger on it, but he was certain that something was going to happen in this building.

He started to having visions that a co-worker's mother was ill. Julie was a nice girl who had connected with Daniel right away. She had never mentioned that her mother was terminally ill, but Daniel somehow knew.

At this time, Daniel was beginning to learn about the various health benefits of gold so he recommended that Julie's mother investigate using gold for healing. He described how Moses had used this biblical mineral by burning particles into an ash to be consumed.

During this period also, Paula began to act out tremendous amounts of jealousy and insecurity. She started to suspect Daniel and Julie to be more than just work friends. I can vouch for the character of Daniel and assure you he did nothing to deserve such accusations.

Some time passed, and Daniel became involved in a group prospecting for gold. They would team up at various parts of the Lehigh River and spend an afternoon panning for gold. He was learning both the medicinal value and the history of this enchanting material.

One day when Daniel showed up for work, a new manager was announced. Daniel immediately got a warm feeling from this new team member. When the new manager went into the stock room to restock the beer coolers, Daniel took the opportunity to offer his assistance and introduce himself.

"My name is Daniel, but most people call me Rocky," Daniel said, reaching out his hand.

"It's a pleasure to meet you," the new manager said. "My name is Michael Lutterschmidt. You can call me Mike."

I have always been able to connect with people and relate to many different walks of life. Being a manager and having a successful sales career before my targeting began molded my confidence around social situations and work-related interactions. Something about Daniel seemed familiar. I could speak to him as if we had been friends all along. He talked about his gold prospecting and related some of his supernatural experiences. He told me he felt a strange vibe in the building. I mentioned to him how I had an unusual feeling when I walked into the stock room, like the air was so heavy I couldn't breathe, but had chalked it up to my mold anxiety.

Since Daniel was open and willing to discuss his personal thoughts with me at work, I decided to confide in him as well. I was deeply into my targeting and was still pissed off that I had been wrongly terminated from my casino job. I told Daniel how I was being stalked and harassed everywhere I went.

"Don't be surprised if you see trucks and creepy white vans with out of state plates sitting in the parking lot watching me all night," I said. I was trying to describe my typical day of organized stalking.

Without me saying another word, Daniel said a white van had been parked outside the whole night.

I smiled with relief. I had been observing that van since it had pulled into the parking lot. When Daniel had confronted the driver, he had sped away. Daniel didn't know what it was all about until I mentioned the organized stalking.

Having someone recognize even a small portion of my covert execution was a saving grace. The van was a tiny fraction of it. I have also been surgically violated with, what I believe to be, body area networking implants. Many of the perpetrators park within fifty yards and torment me with technology.

Daniel and I got to play some games of our own with my demon stalkers. I would send him out with a few complimentary pizza slices and the perturbed drivers would speed away to avoid recognition. Daniel even observed some of the subtle forms of harassment that many people would disregard. We once saw a raven flying around the parking lot ... in center city Allentown? The symbolism was meant for me alone. The Illuminati spares no expense to orchestrate my elaborate, living nightmare. Nonetheless, for reasons dear to me, Daniel witnessed the large symbolic bird.

Ever since the first day that Daniel introduced himself to me, we have connected in ways I cannot explain. I related to Daniel and recognized his knowledge regarding gold and the supernatural without doubt or criticism. In return, Daniel gave me some much-needed recognition for the vehicular stalking I was enduring. For whatever reason, Daniel and I really listened to each other. I would help him do his tasks so he could earn more money, and in return Daniel was there for me with whatever I needed.

Even before we knew each other well, and certainly before we began this journey, we felt a brotherly bond. As the past catches up to the current day with splashes of flashbacks, I can proclaim with confidence that our journey began well before we realized.

No Mercy, No Surrender

Once again, I am being mocked with coincidental nonsense. I explained in Session VI that I get primed with the symbolic number 666. I used session VI to explore automatic writing while attempting to dream walk through this mysterious, guiding energy. Session XI will have a similar theme.

Another brainwashing psyop I get bombarded with every day is the numeral 1111. Some claim the four 1's are good luck—when you catch the clock at 11:11, angels are with you. After diving deeper into the symbolism of my own targeting, I may have discovered 1111 is a biblical passage that translates loosely into "no mercy." As I am suffering excruciating pain, my tormentors prove with unwavering demonstrations that they hold no mercy for my life.

It is very peculiar, how no matter where I am or what I am doing, when the time reads 11:11, I glance at a clock. During that magical minute, something forces me to witness the numerology. Perhaps this "check in" is indeed other worldly communication. Could this be why my tormentors mock the magic by harassing me with those numbers on license plates, shirts, or even smudged on my vehicle?

In this session I will try to demonstrate the synergy between the past and the present. Daniel and I have been led down different roads. Even though the lives we have lived and our traveled paths have been completely different, we both stand here today with the same awareness that people of our world are in grave danger. We both acknowledge that we are not alone in this universe and the secret society governing us is not acting for humanity's greater good.

In my first book, *Extrajudicial Execution*, the chapter "Targeted Individual" captures my life in horrifying detail and describes when I met Daniel for the first time. To stay consistent with our purpose, I will refer you to my previous books to discover how my destiny got me where I am today. I will use this time to capture my life since those published works were written.

Rocky has taught me a lot and I think I taught him some things as well. When we started our journey, I was desperate to escape into another project to distracting my mind from the constant torture. I had a few ideas, though something told me to blindly begin this project with Daniel despite not having an end in mind. I find it comical how I still don't have any idea of a conclusion. Much like sailing on a cloudy day with no compass, we began with no clear direction.

The induced pain had made it impossible to work at a normal job since each day was more painful than the last. I knew Daniel was experimenting with fasting, but it wasn't until I started to write about the cleansing process that I acknowledged the communication. Daniel, or perhaps a higher power working through Daniel, was screaming truth at me.

I joked around with Daniel about why he didn't push me to start fasting with him earlier. He told me, "It is not my place to make you do anything. You need to do it for yourself."

Since I tend to be a smart ass, I responded, "If I had a broken leg and needed to be driven to the emergency room, would you tell me to drive myself?"

Obviously, I needed help recognizing the actual message, considering it took me a few weeks to begin a fasting on my own.

I was a fool for not listening to obvious messages, and Daniel could have been more forthcoming to the seriousness of the situation. My body needed severe cleansing and Rocky knew my health was rapidly declining.

I agree with Rocky that a person needs to accept personal responsibility to better themselves. After all, I just finished preaching about the concept of free will.

I sometimes ponder why Daniel continues to be a dear friend, especially since my own blood brother turned against me. Daniel came into my life for a reason. I know that now. I believe a higher power was insistent that I start cleansing. For whatever the reason, I just wasn't listening at the time.

After a few years of friendship, and now starting this journey, we have somehow discovered a lot more than what we were supposed to acknowledge. Daniel showed me how the paranormal is all around us all the time. I showed Daniel how I am fighting real life monsters hiding within our government.

My dying testimony ended with an unknown, future conclusion. I was falling victim to constant espionage which sabotaged my employment. The goal was to incarcerate me for not being able to pay alimony and support. I have no doubt that if I would have spent just one night behind bars, I would have been killed. I was forced to be creative with my survival tactics and applied for social security disability. I figured that since all my doctors were coerced to play along with my targeting, I could use the fraud to my advantage.

I was approved for benefits based on the diagnosis of paranoid schizophrenia because I told the truth. I told the psychiatrist I had been surgically violated and linked up to a satellite. When I explained how Happy Place and the monsters within our government were paying thousands of people to follow a GPS to torture me with physical and psychological warfare, he quickly concluded I was delusional.

Once I was approved for benefits, the espionage became obsolete. My daughter and I still get $3,400 every month, even though I have not been able to speak to her for over five years. My wife's father, at one time a mob boss, began the process of the systematic destruction of my life. Now that I have no risk of incarceration and refuse to react to the engineered attempts to make me lash out, Lucifer's demons are only left with one alternative— poison me to death.

I have been to every type of doctor and have basically stopped seeking medical help. After hearing an Air Force representative coerce my own doctor into preventing my medical treatment while I was waiting in the adjoining room, I knew I was on my own. Before I started fasting, I was near death. My entire left side, from my temple down to my chest, was smothered by mycoplasma. My neck muscles ached so terribly that tears formed in my eyes.

The silicone-based bio film used in my torment is military grade eugenics with the capability of transmitting and receiving wireless signals. My new connection with guiding communication showed that one of the devices implanted within my body is called Larxen. At the time, I considered this to be coincidental nonsense. But then I started to listen and learned the science behind this particular RFID. The device produces silicone to transmit signals.

My tormentors also use the device to mock my agonizing mold symptoms, torturing me with painful gluey congestion. I am a human experiment, and I assure you Happy Place is selling the live streaming of my life. The technology allows them to see through my eyes, hear through my ears, and record my thoughts. With the effects of these electronic weapons in combination with various biometric devices implanted in me, a kind of crucifixion appears inevitable.

I have also been contributing to my own lethal situation. The stress I have allowed into my life caused me to smoke over a pack a day. I was eating garbage, chugging corn syrup, overloading my body with sugars and carbohydrates. I was basically helping my tormentors poison me to death.

Two weeks after I was supposed to start fasting I got smacked in the face by a power not of this world, figuratively speaking. I remember that day vividly. Something reached inside and shook me to my core. I will attempt to dream walk through my own memories of that recent past.

I woke up on the couch early one morning, heated a left-over cup of coffee and walked outside to sit in my car. The pain from my neck and left side was so intense it triggered a high-pitched humming noise. My neck was so tight I couldn't move without excruciating pain. I sat in my car and tears drip down my face as I contemplated my hopeless state.

I often get attacked in places where I am supposed to feel safe. Inside Lori's apartment, my parents' house, and even hotel rooms I am still harassed. The combination of pain and the psychological stress of not having a sanctuary is designed to steer me to commit suicide or homicide. Almost every morning for the last two weeks, I have found myself trying to ease the torture by sitting in my car. To neighbors, the picture of me sitting in my car probably adds to my image of mental illness.

This morning, the pain reached an all-time high. By about a quarter past five I was down to my last cigarette. The rest of the day was filled with dreadful, military-run street theater. The psychological warfare in combination with the pain was leading up to a dangerous boiling point. I was taunted with little girls the age of my daughter act out skits in front of me. Vehicles surrounded me with DAD stickers, a famous mouse and marines. Their goal was to provoke me with as much evil as possible, triggering a desire to seek justice by my own hands. Since my life is being recorded, if I ever react, my behavior will be used against me. No one will ever see me get provoked, but everyone will watch the video of me reacting to the provocation.

Here is an example of the evil, covert street theater I witness which is designed to make me lash out and react. I was strolling down the dairy section of the grocery store when about fifteen feet ahead of me a woman was standing behind a cart with her ten-year-old daughter inside. The woman gave me a sinister glance then proceeded to violently yank her daughter's hair. Her daughter started crying hysterically, weeping and asking her mom why she had pulled her hair. Tears welled up in my eyes at the cruelty. Someone obviously had paid this woman to pull her daughter's hair in front of me, engineering my tearful emotion. It is not a coincidence that this girl was my daughter's age, and my own daughter was basically kidnapped with lies and corruption.

Recall Daniel's dream when he was fighting possessed people and the demon poured out as he touched them. If Daniel had been with me, I would have made him touch that woman like the demons in his dream. Those maliciously evil actions are at the hands of the Illuminati, and my flashlight is getting brighter with every word.

This is how I catch Lucifer in the true light. The Illuminati is entirely structured around pedophilia. I believe sadistic rituals are meant to worship or summon an evil power. My recent awareness has shown me the truth about my ex-wife's true molester. She once told me she was raped when she was young. It turns out that her father had sacrificed Gena for his own initiation into his local chapter of the Illuminati. The sacrifice of one's own child demonstrates commitment and in return gives the initiate an "untouchable" status, protecting him from the law itself.

What this heinous sacrifice achieves is lifelong slavery. If you ever try to get out or expose its secrets, the Illuminati will crush you. Just ask Justin Bieber how he feels about selling his soul. The Devil's Persuasion, which got the mother to abuse her own daughter in the store, was street theater designed to get a reaction out of me. I am truly at war with Lucifer and his easily duped demons.

These mastermind criminals tell perpetrators that the targeted individual, like me, is worthy of punishment and will commit suicide. But in six out of ten cases, the result of these evil games will be homicide. Perhaps the guiding forces thought I would cause a big scene inside the store, providing more evidence of mental illness. Maybe I was supposed to attack the woman for abusing her daughter. All I did, though, was shed a tear and get incredibly angry.

I knew I needed to start taking better care of myself. I knew it seemed a little too coincidental that I was gravitating toward fasting. Daniel had invited me to start fasting with him, but did I listen? Not only did I ignorantly refuse, but I also felt myself giving up, succumbing to my inevitable, judicial fate.

That afternoon, I awoke a different man as if from a trance. I had quit smoking once before. I was serious about it. I counted the days and treated each one as a victory. I was up to thirty-one days until my ex-wife filed her fifth fraudulent contempt order and I reverted right back to smoking. I allowed a demon to attack my mind. This time, my urge to quit smoking didn't come from me. I felt a fierce responsibility.

I remember getting out of my car and leaning against the side door. The sun was shining on a cool, August afternoon. I looked up toward the sun and closed my eyes. I don't know why I spoke these words or what compelled me to say them with such confidence: "I swear to you, my Holy Father, I will never smoke another cigarette."

I don't bother counting the smoke-free days or keep track of small victories. I didn't have to attend a class or mentally prepare for giving up my smokes. I made a promise to Him and there is no way in Hell I am letting Him down. Now I don't care how many days it has been without a cigarette.

This wasn't the only betterment I decided to take on. To challenge myself further, I committed myself to start fasting that same afternoon. A spiritual empowerment had engulfed my confidence, and I began to blindly act with faith. Daniel would help me prepare for my journey later that evening. He had everything ready for me knowing I would have this awakening. Although I arrived late, Daniel was there patiently waiting.

He gave me two, half-gallon jugs and proceeded to explain the process for making my drinking water. If you were to analyze the drinking water of our city's water supply, you would probably be very disturbed. The amount of lime in Allentown's water supply is appalling. Obviously, there is a process to clean and prepare water for public consumption. But how thorough do you think the process is for decontamination?

Traces of prescribed pharmaceuticals have been found in city water. So just think—when you are pouring water into your kid's oatmeal, your kids are ingesting traces of Viagra and blood thinners. Among the other contaminants found in our water is chlorine, ostensibly added to help purify the water. How healthy do you think that is for you? The secret society wants you to believe that fluoride is intentionally put into our water to prevent tooth decay. There are also several heavy metals and minerals in the water supply that are not all harmless to the human body.

Daniel explained how I would be drinking gallons of purified water so the cleansing would adequately work. First, I would boil the water for several minutes. Even though our water is purified by city standards, microbes, bacteria, and parasites can still be prevalent. Boiling the water eliminates anything biologically harmful. Then, I would let the water stand and return to room temperature to allow the chemicals to steam themselves out of the water.

I skipped the next step due to lack of freezer space. You are supposed to freeze the water. As the ice thaws, the heavy metals, minerals and fluoride get pulled into the ice as the pure water freely melts away.

Once my water was ready, Daniel gave me four ingredients to add to my drinking water. I took each half-gallon jug and added a pinch of dead sea salt followed by a pinch of food-grade Epson salt. I was preparing to replace my diet with water, so maintaining electrolytes in my system was crucial.

Next, I added a half teaspoon of baking soda. Most baking soda products contain aluminum, so please do your research. Ingesting small quantities of aluminum for extended periods of time could be very harmful. Sodium bicarbonate helps balance the body's Ph level, preventing acidity from building up. Cancer fungus, and parasites thrive in high acidic environments, so a steady balance of baking soda and high energy foods will make your system uninhabitable for fungus, candida and harmful bacteria.

The last step was to add a pinch of borax to help aid in the cleansing process. Borax does a few different things. First, it helps break down any current fungal or bacterial infections. Borax will help eliminate Morgellons, parasites and even cancer. Another benefit to small yet steady quantities of borax is the effect it has on the pineal gland. Your third eye can become corroded with calcium, heavy metals and a gluey film from corn syrup, fructose and fats. Whether this is deliberate is another topic. Borax helps to decalcify the pineal gland, strengthening the other five senses.

I have stopped smoking. I have stopped eating red meat, bread or desserts. For the first two days of fasting I only drank water. Today, my daily diet consists of nearly two gallons of my special water. If I eat, I eat an avocado, homemade hummus, or some fruits and vegetables. I thought I would miss red meat, bread and desserts, but when the cleansing began to physically show positive signs, I received a new perspective. My taste buds started to rejuvenate themselves and I felt as if I were tasting everything again for the first time. Eating a banana now seems like I was in a paradise resort. The taste of a juicy, ripe pear hits every sensory on my palate and I have received a newfound respect for raw foods. I have begun to maximize all five senses.

To celebrate the changes in my life, I have decided that moving forward with my writing I will now call Daniel by the fond name I have been calling him from the beginning—Rocky.

After three days of fasting, I called Rocky and told him I was having terrible stomach pains. For two days, I had suffered from painful constipation. Rocky insisted I come over. We had planned to start another session, but the pain in my stomach had now moved to my lower back as well. Rocky made me drink a glass of warm water with four tablespoons of baking soda. I was relieved when I forced down the final drop, not because the pain had subsided, but because I was done with that horrible taste. Then, of course, Rocky prepared another glass of sodium bicarbonate water to chug. After I struggled through swallowing the chalky nastiness, we sat on the couch and watched a show. Within an hour, I felt painful churning in my stomach.

I excused myself to the bathroom and Rocky chuckled as I got up. After a few violent bowel outbursts, the toilet was filled with a black tar and no matter how many times I flushed, the black residue stuck to the toilet. Rocky told me my system had been close to failing.

By the next day I was somewhat relieved. I went over to Rocky's so we could get some work done, but Rocky had a different idea. I was on my fourth day of fasting and he knew it was time to acknowledge the spiritual effects of cleansing. He prepared incense and herbs, and we convened in his backyard under a small trellis of grape vines woven above our heads.

Rocky asked me to kneel and pray. Then he ignited a charcoal brick and put frankincense, myrrh, mug-wart and a few other biblical incenses on the burning briquette. He told me to put my hands together and press them against my forehead. The open triangle between my hands created a pocket for the smoke to linger. Rocky asked me to pray and breathe in the smoldering, ancient aromas.

So… I prayed. I wasn't sure what to pray for, or even how to pray. As the warm smoke filled my lungs, my mind drifted away from my body. I found myself speaking to a power I could not see nor hear but felt with every fiber of my being. Instead of my thoughts wandering around about my own pain and suffering, I began to think about the millions of children who have been sold, tortured and murdered. I thought about my daughter and all the injustice in the world. I imagined the pain and torture of my fellow targeted individuals. Tears began to stream down my face.

I am not sure how to explain what I felt as I knelt there and prayed over biblical smoke. Within those ten minutes, though, I gave myself entirely to my Holy Father. My overwhelming sadness came from acknowledging the evil in our world. In that moment of prayer, without words, I was told to "continue."

I asked my Holy Father what I could do to save the world from such horrific plots and rituals. Then I felt a sense of courage flow though me. With each breath, I began to fill my chest with more air. A confidence came over me that I have never felt before. I did not receive instructions on what to do next. I still don't have a clue how I am supposed to prevent millions of children from being abused or how to save the entire human race from being enslaved. But I was told to continue. That evening, while on my knees, I felt the weight of the world though I also felt myself holding the world steady with pure will and resilience.

Accepting my responsibility to continue, I made the sign of the cross and said "Amen," as one last tear dripped from my cheek.

Rocky put his hand on my back. "Just relax and take your time. Speaking with Him can be overwhelming."

I stood up but had a hard time reconnecting with my current self. I remember being quiet and hearing Rocky talking from a distance, which seemed far away. I was unsure of where I had just been. Part of my mind was still floating in another world.

The more Rocky spoke, the more his words pulled me back. I was just four days into my fast and I was intimately infatuated with it. Rocky was about to show me how to willfully control my own out-of-body experience.

We walked over and sat alongside each other on a garden wall. I was still rallying my consciousness, so I was only hearing half of what he was telling me. I knew he was teaching me a breathing exercise.

When Rocky asked if I was ready, I said, "Wait… what?"

"Just follow me," Rocky replied.

This is what I learned. In the first phase, you take five deep breaths, inhaling violently through my nose no matter how embarrassing the noise. You inhale until you have filled every possible space in your lungs. Then, with an equally violent outburst through your mouth, you force the air out so aggressively that your neighbors would hear whooshing wind.

I remember all kinds of crap breaking up and dripping out of my mouth. Rocky told me not to worry and keep going. After the five deep breaths, you take five aggressive short breaths and then exhaled through the nose. After the last short breath is exhaled, you take a calming deep breath in through the nasal passages and out through the mouth.

During this last step, while slowly blowing out the air, I somehow opened a doorway. A euphoric calmness rushed through my body. When the last of the air was exhaled, I proceeded with another set of five aggressive deep breaths.

This is when we heard the neighbors come outside. The breathing exercise wasn't a calm meditation, but rather an obnoxious, unsanitary cleansing. We could feel the neighbor's eyes on our backs. We didn't care what anyone thought, so we continued as if we were alone on top of a mountain.

After the fifth violent exhalation, we did five more short breaths as before. For the final step, we took in the deepest breath we could possibly muster and held it tightly while clenching our muscles. Starting with the sphincter, we clenched every muscle in our body one at a time. As we squeezed our buttocks, we made gripping fists and tightened our stomachs, backs, legs and arms. When we could barely hold the breath any longer, we squeezed our eyes shut and tightened every facial muscle. Then, with a sudden relief, we blew out our air and released our clenched muscles. When the air left my lungs and my muscles relaxed, I felt like my spirit was venturing out of that door I had somehow opened.

The breathing method was painful and disturbing. I was aware enough to know the neighbors were outside watching us—and to know some nasty bio shit was breaking up and fleeing my body.

The process was indeed exercise. It wasn't until I had held my breath and clenched my muscles, however, that I began to feel the spiritual connection. Considering that this feeling may have come from outside this world, words are difficult to find for an adequate description of the experience. But I'll try anyway.

A euphoric feeling rushed through my body as I was clenching my muscles and holding in my breath. It was like an orgasm, though every muscle in my body climaxed all at once. My brain tingled with a purifying vibration. I suspect that some people who suffer from addiction might chase this euphoric feeling unnaturally. The out-of-body experience occurred when I was halfway through exhaling that last enormous breath. The more air I released, the more I felt myself drift away.

I remember sitting on the wall with Rocky on my left. I saw myself fall backward onto the grass while I sat there watching myself fall. Once my body hit the grass, I was gone. But I didn't know I was gone until a while later because for twenty-three minutes I was somewhere else. After those twenty-three minutes, of which I have no memory, I opened my eyes and found myself lying down. Where did I go after I hit the grass? If this was my own spirit, why can't I remember?

I propped myself up and rubbed my eyes. I looked at Rocky and he was sitting still as a statue in the same position as when we had started.

"Are you OK?" Rocky asked.

I responded with a question of my own. "What happened?"

He said he watched me fall backward, though neither of us realized we had lost those twenty-three minutes until we had come back inside and seen the clock.

I believe I traveled somewhere. I imagine I was standing in space having a conversation. I don't know who I spoke to or where I went. Maybe my mind somehow tapped into astral projection and I traveled in time. Wondering why I can't remember who I spoke with, what was said or where I was for those twenty-three minutes is as mind boggling as the concept of time travel. Perhaps the reason

I cannot remember is because those twenty-three minutes hadn't happened yet.

I sat back up and my entire body felt numb. Rocky suggested we go inside, and I stumbled behind him, meandering into the kitchen where Rocky asked me to kneel. He anointed my head with holy oil while making the sign of the cross, and then he placed his palm on my head and began to ask our Holy Father to bless me. I don't recall the words he spoke. I was self-absorbed, pondering my out-of-body experience and how it related to the message I had received earlier: "Continue."

Blind faith has since taken over my life. I know I have been legally elected for experimentation and extrajudicial execution without a clue as to the reason. The current law lists the methods for execution under law ICD-9-CM E978 performed at the behest of the judiciary or ruling authority {whether permanent or temporary} as: asphyxiation by gas, beheading by guillotine, capital punishment, electrocution, hanging, poisoning, shooting, or other specified means. Read my first book and learn what Happy Place considers "other means." Then read my second book and ask yourself why a previous administration ordered thirty thousand guillotines, which have been distributed to numerous FEMA camps.

Unfortunately, seeing the world through my eyes desensitizes my emotions to life's mortality. I feel an overwhelming responsibility that I have something important to accomplish. I am following a plan that I do not fully acknowledge or understand. And I am supposed to continue?

One morning before dawn, I was sitting in my car seeking refuge from inside DEW (direct energy weapon) attacks. I gazed up at the waning moon and the two bright stars shining on either side. I remember the warmth from my cup of hot water made the cool breeze more soothing. I closed my eyes and wondered, *Why do I see what I see?* People today are too willing to participate in the Devil's Persuasion. Is there a reason why so much energy has been focused on putting my torture and crucifixion on the public stage?

I picked up my phone and felt a kind of auto pilot take control. I started writing, though it seemed like someone else was using my body to type the words. Here is the message that was automatically written.

Ignore his Demons, and look up to the sky.
I do feel your pain, and it's alright to cry.
My world is suffering, with Evil and Sin,
Which is why I sent you, and it's time to begin.
For far too long, I have been ignored.
A false light has sprouted, and now is adored.
My creation is lost, misguided and dark.
I need you to shine, for you are my spark.
You have my power, you have my light.
Fight through this pain, with all your might.
When your job is done, you will be free.
I won't let them take you, you belong with me.
It may seem impossible, truly unreal.
But too many people, took a Devil's deal.
Witness the evil, how my children are gone.
Consumed by demons, intentionally wrong.
No need for justice, revenge or a gun.
I need you to Scribe and shine like the sun.
Your role is to suffer, and awaken my gift.
For these powers of evil, will soon be adrift.
As it is written, it must be so.
Use my words, and your pen will flow.
You have my gift, you have my love.
Now fly like an Angel, and soar like a Dove.

I once wrote that God will not come down to save us. God gave each of us the power to save ourselves. I just wish that power came with instructions. Then I think about Rocky. He didn't have instructions to get rid of the terrifying shadow entity. He relieved Paula and his son from harassing entities after speaking through the phone, demanding they leave his family alone. I don't believe Rocky received instructions about how to control the paranormal, though he confidently acts when necessary. From what I can determine, Rocky first acknowledges, then believes, and then acts with faith.

I now try to live my life according to the message, "Continue." I started fasting, so I continue. I started writing, so I continue. I survived by ignoring the evil street theater, so I continue to ignore demons. Although seeking medical help for the excruciating pain has been disappointing and discouraging, I continue using a process of fasting and I will continue to shine a spotlight on my covert torture.

Rocky and I started this project with no direction or any specific end in mind, yet we continue to blindly travel down this road. I have already shared some disturbing realities that you may find impossible to be true. I will continue to share the dark perceptions of the world through my eyes. I admit to my own contradictions, which is my process of building stronger perceptions.

Allow me to boost my credibility a bit. In my last book, I wrote that the Bermuda Triangle has a strange energy that is responsible for the disappearance of several planes and ships. My intuition was proven accurate by the recent revelation that an enormous crystal pyramid has been made public on the ocean floor in the center of the Bermuda Triangle.

When I spoke in previous books about monsters, you might have thought I was referring to sick, demented people. Although this is partly true, I wish reality were that simply. Rocky has opened my life up to the paranormal. We have otherworldly entities, both good and evil, all around us in the world. Some entities want to communicate and possibly help us. Other forms of supernatural energy may try to instill fear or even harm us. Considering all the unexplained stories I have described so far, I hope you are being awakened to some new perceptions.

Our world has been inhabited by monsters long before man walked the Earth. The term monster is used loosely. When I think of a dinosaur standing twenty-five feet tall with razor sharp teeth, I consider to be a monster. I consider the Loch Ness Monster the same, but maybe this ancient aquatic mammal is the friendliest, most intelligent creature on the planet—I don't know. Perhaps we can't prove the creature exists because the monster is smart enough to know its own survival depends upon its secrecy. Think about how we consider dolphins, seals, and otters to be friendly pets of the water. Loch Ness could have the same charming character.

I use the term monster to describe anything that is not human and could be harmful to people. Consider all the monsters we know exist and which have ceased to exist. Dinosaurs, saber tooth tigers, thirty-foot python, and sharks are obvious examples. What about the fifty-foot-tall giants that were oddly left out of our history books? Skeletal remains have been unearthed revealing enormous, humanlike creatures. The size alone could be dangerous, no matter how gentle the Giant. Perhaps the giants were Nephilim, offspring of God sent to protect the Kingdom of Heaven. Maybe these giants were just a genetic experiment from a more advanced life form. Obviously, they died out, and all evidence of their existence was literally buried.

The rake has been captured on video, and this half-man, half-canine creature is frightening. The population recently went through a vampire fad. Fiction is fact. Since medieval times, entire armies have been conscripted for the sole purpose of fighting vampires, which brings me to my next monster.

Several species of alien life are living among us. Some are curious and helpful. Other life forms are actively involved in the evil we are witnessing suffocate humanity. I am starting to believe the dracnoids and the reptilians are Lucifer's demons. These ancient, AI-subservient life forms are trying to turn the human species into transhumans—half-technology, half-human. Unfortunately, these monsters are far more advanced and have fooled the population by impersonating our own kind using plasma technology and bioengineering.

My previous books helped to expose a group of ancient monsters for abducting millions of children to be harvested for their blood. These monsters contribute to the world's infestation of Illuminati and are the enemies I'm at war with today. The Trojan Horse they hide behind has come close to enslaving the world by infiltrating our governments, societies and the minds of humans through using technology and the Devil's Persuasion. This global conglomerate I call Happy Place has grown to a power that is incalculable.

I have discovered the blood line of this monstrosity stems back to a time of gods and giants. Jinns are clever monsters that send their victims into a dream world while drinking them dry. You can see little kids and their families idolizing these monsters but try to see the reality from my eyes. Happy Place and the family members behind it were Nazi sympathizers. The CIA helped Happy Place achieve the land they currently occupy, and they also have been granted the privilege of governing themselves to conveniently hide their Nazi-inspired human experimentation. These Nazi necromancers are ancient monsters worshiping dark lords of Saturn.

Kids today are carrying around their favorite stuffed animal mouse while their parents willingly give these monsters money and power. The Jinn of our world today have put the population into a dream world. While these monsters are mocking us with entertaining movies and hidden smut, the Trojan Horse is processing millions of children to be raped, tortured and killed.

I am not being tortured to death because I use women or I am a drug addict. I simply refuse to stop exposing the true faces of these monsters. I was told to continue. So, I continue.

Review some of the entities Rocky has dealt with. Even though the shadow figures aren't blood sucking vampires, a dark entity physically terrified Pedro and then the entire family upstairs. Since it was able to bring harm to people, I classify that shadow figure as a monster.

As if dealing with the various monsters isn't hard enough, we also must deal with people who act like monsters. When my neighbors are paid to attack me with science fiction weaponry or when paid perpetrators attack me with street theater, they are allowing the Devil's Persuasion to turn them into demons. I need Rocky with me to touch these possessed people and cleanse them of the demon inside.

To help me compartmentalize the overwhelming truths of the world, I began to use a form of yoga to meditate in a way which connects my body and mind. The deeply cleansing ritual of stretching and breathing must have been downloaded to me from another world. I don't know any other way to explain how I know the meditating routine I practice. I can consider my memories from yoga on the Nintendo Wii and how Rocky learned to fight during his dreams. With all honesty, I believe I have a power showing me what I need to do. Since this power cannot be seen or substantiated, finding the right words will be challenging. Whatever the explanation, I feel stronger and more in control since my daily meditating ritual.

I practice my breathing and each day I learn how better to control the experience. The first time, when I fell onto the grass, I had no idea what to expect and it caught me off guard. The next few times, my mind was conditioned to be scared. When I felt my mind being pulled away, my body shook itself away from falling, preventing a similar out-of-body experience. The more I practice, the more I can drop the fear, let myself go, and embrace the journey.

Perhaps I am getting a glimpse of some purpose. Rocky experiences some dark entities in addition to spiritual connections. In several situations, Rocky has demonstrated the ability to control some kinds of paranormal energy. He may have come into my life to keep me alive and fighting. I can't control monsters within our government, but I can make sure people do their jobs within our government. I can scream truth so loudly, action becomes necessary. My pen truly is my sword.

Many eyes and cameras are watching me, and this attention creates an enormous amount of energy. How can I harness this energy and use it for the greater good? Remember how Daniel got inspired by the guitar-playing Bible teacher? Brother Jake had an ugly scar, though Daniel only noticed that Brother Jake was genuinely happy and grateful.

The Lord said to Daniel, "Do you see?" Maybe my role was to be wrongly accused and tortured on the public stage so I can give my audience a similar message: "I can be tortured with a daunting fate, yet still demonstrate love and hope. I can continue to take care

of my body, mind, and spirit despite the induced, agonizing pain."
Whatever the purpose or how we conclude, I will continue.

These last few weeks have been excruciatingly painful. I am
following the process of fasting, but the induced pain and brutal
psychological warfare is relentless. Events recently took place that
I cannot overlook.

One day, Rocky randomly asked me to look at some paperwork
he had received from court. While highly intelligent, Daniel is a
bit deficient in some areas. When I opened the envelope, I realized
Rocky had been ignoring some serious charges. One night he had
thrown a bag of trash in a dumpster near his house. Apparently,
someone called the police and filed criminal charges. Rocky was
being charged with theft of services for throwing away a bag of
trash.

I helped him fill out the paperwork and quickly took him to
get his fingerprints taken. He was running out of time. The day of
the hearing arrived, and Rocky waited with Paula and me in the
magistrate's office. The police officer walked in and I instantly felt
a familiar streak of anger. I recognized the officer from my daily
targeting and street theater.

The cop lied to the judge about some previous charges. The
entire legal procedure seemed peculiar and I wondered why Rocky
had been charged for such a minor offense in the first place. What if
he would have ignored that legal notice, missed the hearing, and a
bench warrant would have been issued? Because he threw a bag of
trash into a dumpster? These kinds of disruptive legal accusations
are often part of COINTELPRO.

I spoke to the judge on Daniel's behalf. I was able to get him a
public defender for an upcoming trial. I also gave the judge a copy
of my previous books to "continue" spreading the truth.

Rocky was on unemployment, much like so many others,
because of a false flag COVID-19 pandemic. Then his employer
called and said they were going to start bringing people back
into work. He worked for a couple days, then something strange
happened. A manager told Rocky he had to work on the traveling

team or there would be no other opportunities. Rocky had to travel to Tennessee for a few weeks and then Alabama for a few more.

Before Rocky started his travel, we were making incredible progress with our process. My dream walking became so vivid I felt like I was standing alongside Rocky while we traveled back in time. The way these sessions are moving forward is creating greater awareness.

But now Rocky's job has changed with no other options preventing us from expanding these sessions—at least in person. So, why do I feel both a paranormal and a real-life force may be trying to prevent us from continuing? Are we getting too close to a purpose?

Naturally Medicinal

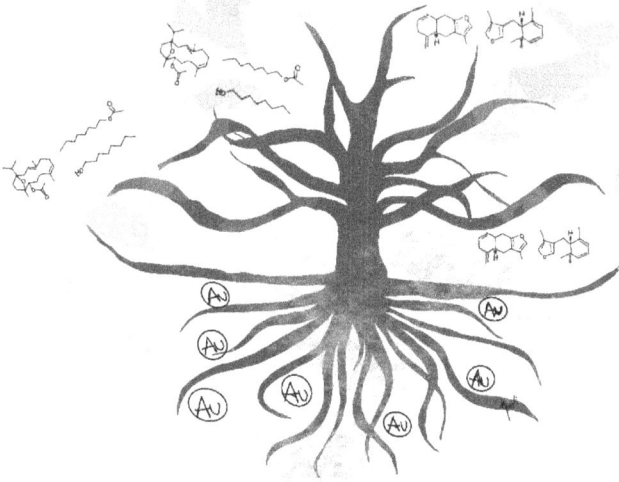

As I begin session twelve, I will continue to mesh together pieces of the past to bring us to the present time. Rocky and I had several adventures since we became friends.. Some were funny, like our windy, rain drenched camping trip. Other adventures were enchanting. We explored creeks along the Lehigh River searching for gold and conducted several paranormal investigations. Rocky and I would spend the next few years creating energy which would later guide us to putting our stories on paper.

I am about a month into my first fasting and I feel amazing, except for the excruciating pain from the implanted torture devices. Since the rest of my body is clear and pure, I can pinpoint exactly the source of the pain. The rest of my body and mind are well. So, with all things considered, Mrs. Lincoln, how was the play?

If I hadn't started cleansing when I did, I might not be around to write these words. Maybe fasting will keep me alive long enough to finish what I was told to continue. When you detox your body, mind and spirit, you can see the world around you more vividly. I am receiving tremendous inspiration, weighing more towards responsibility. I feel it is important to describe some examples of natural healing that have been pushed out of our memories over the course of history.

Before our trillion-dollar pharmaceutical industry poisoned our minds, many cultures used natural medicine. Gold, frankincense and myrrh are probably the most well-known examples from the scriptures. In my last book of rambles, I dedicated a few words to gold and prospecting. So as to not sound repetitive, I will just add on to those thoughts.

Rocky first started to research gold for its monetary value. He joined a prospecting club and dedicated a great deal of time to learning about the history of gold. While he was researching well known geologists and prospectors, he came across a video.

Algorithms are used today for marketing purposes and videos stop being offered if no action is taken. Even though Rocky ignored the video for a long time, something wanted Rocky to watch its content. The video discussed using the element *Au* for medicinal purposes, supporting my claim that important communication is all around us. I don't believe it was the monetary gain that made Rocky interested in gold. Some worldly power wanted him to learn a larger lesson.

Sister Karen once told Daniel to seek answers in the Bible, so he did. Moses, the Prince of Egypt, was an alchemist. He learned how to burn gold and other precious metals into a medicinal ash. When Moses's sister was cast out of the group for seven days and seven nights after falling ill to leprosy, he used silver and myrrh to cure her illness.

When Moses climbed Mount Sinai to receive the commandments, he knew he didn't have much food or water when he departed on his forty-day quest. Remember, the fasting opens spiritual doorways, and something tells me the purity of body, mind and spirit allowed Moses to receive the word of God.

Ask yourself how Moses learned to become an alchemist and understand natural healing. It's not like he had YouTube videos or even a library to consult. Moses just set off to climb up a mountain with no food or water. Blind faith was guiding this man.

Now think about the time Rocky ordered the troll to leave his room. Think about when he prayed for the shadow entity to stop terrorizing the family upstairs. Think about the cancerous tumor shrinking after Rocky willed it away. How does Rocky know what to do and how to do the things he did?

The theme of gold continues in the story of Moses. Moses's people thought he would not return from his quest. So, they decided to make a new god, literally. A golden calf was created to represent a god. Moses was furious when he came back famished and saw them honoring a golden idol. He smashed the tablets containing the Ten Commandments in a raging tantrum.

I would be upset too if I had just spent forty days on top of a mountain with no food or shelter receiving guidance from God only to come back down and find my people praying to a statue. He pushed the golden calf into the fire, burnt it down to ash, and mixed the medicine into their drinking water. When the people complained the water was bitter, everyone thought it was their punishment for worshiping a false God. The bitterness was their saving grace. Then, Moses went back up the mountain to apologize and endure another forty days without much food or water.

The Ark of the Covenant was made to keep the word of God safe and keep people safe from the word of God. Stories were written about how a single touch of the Ark could burn a person to ashes. Special gloves and garments were needed and only the chosen ones could handle the power. Do you know what magical material this Holy filing cabinet was made of? You have probably guessed—gold-plated wood.

The power once contained within the Ark of The Covenant creates a cornucopia of possibilities. UFOs have been captured on video flying over the location of the Ark of the Covenant, which we believe was a power generator of some kind. Certainly, the power could have had an extraterrestrial source, or it could have been the power of God. Large crystals were discovered at the site of the Roswell crash that could power an entire electrical grid. Also, consider that Moses divided the Red Sea. I once watched Rocky create ripples on the surface of the water with his thoughts. And he taught me how to move a pinwheel by asking it to move. The human mind contains more abilities than we realize. Is that the power of God coming out through us in his image?

Since gold is expensive today, Rocky started to practice making medicine from other precious metals, herbs, roots, salts and oils. The colloidal silver products available on the shelf are not pure, so Rocky learned how to make it himself. For months, he suffered from a rash between his legs. The doctors prescribed ointment, steroids and creams, but nothing seemed to cure the rash. After one day of applying his own colloidal silver solution a few times, the rash completely disappeared by the next day.

So, why are doctors pumping us full of nonsense when simple, natural medicine often works better anyway? An even better question is: Why are the elites torturing children to drink adrenochrome blood when they can achieve the same medicinal effects using a combination of gold, frankincense and myrrh? The false light is allowing the Devil's Persuasion to mock us in plain sight.

Colloidal gold has rejuvenating properties. It has soothing and harmonizing effects on the body, mind and spirit. Gold promotes a feeling of increased energy, will power, mental focus and libido. The use of gold salts in the treatment of disease was called chrysotherapy in the late 1800s after it was discovered how compounds of gold could hinder the growth of bacillus, which causes tuberculosis. Some gold compounds can be processed by the body and have anti-inflammatory properties. Sodium aurothiomalate and auranofin are common prescriptions for arthritis. The healing abilities of gold go far beyond physical.

Gods ingested gold, wore it, drank from it, slept in it and were buried in gold for a reason. After the examination of several Egyptian mummies, fragments of gold were found collected around the spinal cord. This proves the Egyptians were ingesting gold as medicine. Fort Knox has "shoot on sight" orders to protect the nation's gold reserves. America left a gold leaf pendant on the moon. The tops of pyramids and obelisks were often covered in gold. Niche businesses are now thriving from breaking down old computers to gather the gold from circuit boards. Do you think it is a coincidence we have witnessed a remarkable advancement in technology while gold is being extracted from that same tech? Our currency is supposedly backed by the element *Au*.

The day on which I am writing these words is the day I found a key piece to my puzzle. I have continued fasting and taking care of my body and mind. I continue writing despite being blind to a conclusion. Even though the multiple attempts to seek medical relief have been frustrated by demon activity, I continue to follow the process.

Today I just received a few labs back from my doctor, and the results of cultures from my left sinus gave me goosebumps—moderate Bacillus growth. I instantly opened my notebook and searched for the writing I had done yesterday. There, written by my own hand, was my answer: "Gold could hinder the growth of bacillus, which causes tuberculosis."

If I weren't listening to the message, I would have given up looking for medical help. Maybe I have finally got medical proof of my poisonings and guidance about how to stay alive.

Almost all ancient cultures around the world—from Asia and Egypt to the Mayans—have all obsessed over gold. These ancient civilizations were making medicine to live long, healthy lives. It has been written Moses lived to be 120 years old. When he confronted Pharaoh, he was already 80 years old. My guess is that gold added to his longevity.

So, why the hell are we allowing little kids to suffer with cancer? Why do we let our senior citizens suffer the pain of arthritis? If gold can cure leprosy and help Moses live to such an old age, why are we currently shutting down the world for some engineered virus?

Everything is a lie—but why?

The other two biblical medicines I mentioned are frankincense and myrrh. Myrrh is used for indigestion, ulcers, colds, coughs, asthma, lung congestion, arthritis, cancer, leprosy, spasms and even syphilis. This ancient tree sap has been known to increase the menstrual flow as well, promoting humanity.

Frankincense is also a biblical tree sap that has anti-inflammatory effects and may help relieve osteoarthritis and rheumatoid arthritis. The medicinal properties of this sap improve gut function, asthma and work as a decongestant. Many renowned figures used frankincense for daily routines such as oral health and recognizes its ability to kill cancer.

A remarkable thought has just exploded in my brain. Gold, frankincense and myrrh possess anti-inflammatory properties. They help combat diseases, common ailments, and even cure cancer. I have stated many times already that cancer is just a fungus.

I am in this war with the Illuminati because of fungus. I was born with a genetic susceptibility to mycotoxins found on certain indoor black molds. The illness that devastated my life and nearly took my last breath is known as CIRS, or chronic inflammatory response syndrome.

After my wife insisted we buy a bigger house, we bought one that was contaminated with mold and my genetic susceptibility to fungus led me to this very dangerous condition. I think my genetic susceptibility to this biblical bioweapon was the Lord's way of waking me up to my destiny. The genetic nightmare has helped me realize that the Illuminati is trying to genetically alter our spirituality by using a vaccine to remedy an intentional pandemic.

Dream walk with me for a minute. Take a deep cleansing breath, block out all other distractions, and try to envision my thoughts, seeing through my eyes. I cannot verbally explain some of the truths I have uncovered. I want to try and provide an example of how I see the world differently than most people. I will use the most outrageous example.

We have all heard about the JFK assassination and most people understand there was a conspiracy. But somehow I have seen Jackie Kennedy delivering the fatal shot. If you watch the video footage in extreme zoom and slow motion, you will see a black object in Jackie's right hand. Once the shot is fired, Jackie's hand twitches and I can see her tossing the gun behind the car. If you look at John's head movement in relation to Jackie's right hand, you may agree with the way my intuition adjoins the puzzle pieces. The magic just comes to me. Jackie's behavior after the shot was fired was not entirely natural. Jackie climbed onto the trunk of the car in a robotic, desensitized fashion.

Somehow, this is what I see. I believe the CIA or a secret society needed to prevent JFK from exposing a plot to enslave every man, woman and child. Using personally intimate relationships and provocative photographs as propaganda, they brainwashed Jackie. The CIA used betrayal and their own ideology to convince Jackie to do the unthinkable.

Before that infamous Texas drive, the CIA had Jackie simulate the entire experience dozens of times, acting out each motion and emotion. You may see a frightened woman climb on the back of the car after the shot was fired. I see a desensitized woman acting out a robotic response that was simulated multiple times beforehand. There was only one camera angle. She tossed the gun quickly, almost like she had practiced doing it several times. An appointed service criminal was assigned to retrieve the gun and the conspirators blamed Oswald for the kill whether he was a good marksman or not. Eventually, the truth will come out and you will remember these words.

That being said, my perceptions are often unique, and they cause me to note that these biblical medicines—gold, frankincense and myrrh—all have anti-inflammatory properties that cure diseases, help with various common ailments and are used for preventative care.

The genetic illness that devastated my life—CIRS—is brought on by overexposure to mold and bacteria found in water-damaged buildings. This genetic curse dragged me to the fiery pits of Hell, and when I managed to climb out, Lucifer followed.

It was not a fruit that poisoned the Garden of Eden. The Devil's Persuasion coerced Eve to bite a forbidden mushroom, and a fungus poisoned our land. Gold, frankincense and myrrh are just a few natural medicines that can help us battle the inflammatory fungus infecting the true light. I have been writing about the various types of otherworldly communication and now with my own words, I am getting guidance to heal myself from Lucifer's viciously evil poisonings.

Before we continue with other natural medicine, I want you to ponder why we have drifted toward a dependency with chemical healing rather than the herbs and resources of our ancient past? I don't speak too frequently about Agenda 21, but you must see how evil forces have put population strategies into practice. The earth is a big place. Who the hell gets to decide which group of people get eradicated?

We have learned that Daniel survived for weeks with just water and little food. I lost fourteen pounds since I started fasting and I feel like I could fight a war. Obviously, Moses went eighty days—the first forty to get the word and then another forty days of fasting to get another copy (otherwise we wouldn't have the Ten Commandments after the first tablets were destroyed.) We throw away enormous amounts of food as a society, yet we still have people starving.

The arrogant monsters within our government claim we need to limit the consumption of resources on the planet. So, some idiot listens to a pitch from another idiot to engineer HIV, Corona-19 and Lord only knows what other extermination tactics. It is all a lie. A human being could live a long, healthy life with just one balanced meal per day. So, we are throwing incredible amounts of resources away, yet claim we are devouring too much.

Millions of people will be murdered to satisfy the secret society's population control strategy. Elites will stay fat and happy from our blood, sweat and tears. Hear my words, see through my eyes, and help me prevent our free will from being banished.

Colloidal silver is an antibacterial agent and a topical wound dressing. Some people claim it can cure a cold faster, heal the body better and even treat cancer or HIV. I used colloidal silver to counter the constant bio attacks. Perhaps using colloidal silver is a contributing factor to my survival. Silver has also been used for the tops of obelisks and honored as a precious metal.

Another amazing element is platinum which increases brain function and helps cleanse the pineal gland.

The medicinal properties of copper are often overlooked. The first year I started to hang out with Rocky, I came over to his Allentown apartment and watched him grind copper into a powder. He told me he was making medicine. At the time, I didn't pay too much attention to that statement. We weren't close friends yet.

Copper is an essential nutrient for the body. Together with iron, it enables the body to form red blood cells. It helps maintain healthy bones, blood vessels, nerves and immune function, and it contributes to iron absorption. Sufficient copper in the diet may help prevent cardiovascular disease and osteoporosis. I believe there was a reason we started using copper pipes for drinking water.

The use of copper has anti-aging and skin benefits. It can be used as an antibacterial and anti-inflammatory agent, it fights parasites and promotes good circulation. Copper has been said to stimulate cognitive abilities and, once again, it is a common element that has been claimed to kill cancer.

Keep in mind that 600,000 people die from cancer each year in this country alone, that big pharma is a trillion-dollar industry, and that the Elites are drinking adrenochrome blood for the same medicinal effects found within ancient herbs and metals.

If I am doing my job as a scribe, you should be able to see the false light, a vision of Hell on Earth. Much like everything else on earth, the benefits from some precious metals are countered by the dangers of other metals. Mercury can do a great deal of damage to the brain and some believe it is the cause of autism. Lead has had its share of bad publicity with paint and toys being recalled. Many believe that the chem trails of aircraft consist of aluminum to turn people into walking transmitters.

Another naturally occurring medicinal gift for our defenses is mug-wart. I used to chuckle every time Rocky said the name because it reminded me of Harry Potter. Mug-wart was used in ancient times for rituals and health. Warriors and soldiers used to put mug-wart on their sandals to keep their feet from hurting. The plant could be ingested or inhaled to trigger spiritual experiences, out-of-body experiences and time travel. Mug-wart was one of the smoldering aromas I breathed during my prayer. When I reflect on my own experience with mug wart, I received a spiritual message to "continue" and lost track of twenty-three minutes when I left my body.

Ormus is a beneficial alkaline mineral supplement that supports health and spiritual wellness. Ormus is orbitally rearranged monoatomic elements. Shilajit is a sticky substance found primarily in the rocks of the Himalayas. This is another natural supplement from plants that can promote positive health.

Ashwagandha root is said to enlighten spirituality as well as helping ease anxiety and stress. The medicinal benefits of this root prevent diabetes and break down bacterial and fungal infections. The root can help prevent seizures, block DhT, promote thyroid hormone function, and even cure erectile dysfunction. And once again, this common natural herb is used in the treatment of cancer. So, when a middle-aged man goes to the doctor for erectile dysfunction, will the physician prescribe a blue pill or a root?

It has now been over a week and I cannot get a doctor to return my phone calls about the various bacteria and fungus found on my sinus cultures. I have faith that a higher power is giving me the help I need with every word I type. I am truly inspired—I am no longer looking for help. I believe I am the help.

We can find extremely beneficial medicine right in our back yards. Stinging nettles improve urinary health, help with various skin conditions, relieve arthritis pain and aid in reproductive health. This common herb also improves cardiovascular health, lowers blood sugar, provides allergy relief, boosts the skeletal system and stimulates healthy hair. Do you really believe doctors are offering this root as a remedy to help patients? What the hell are we doing to ourselves? Even more frightening, is it all intentional?

When I was trying to find ways to break up the bio films and Morgellons from my mold illness, I tried everything until I realized the poisoning was intentional. I tried Jensen violet which is a blue oil from a flower. It is used as an antiseptic and a doctor recommended I put a few drops in saline nose spray. Black walnut oil is a wonderful anti-fungal as well as tea tree oil and Cannabis oil. One sniff from peppermint oil and congestion melts away.

I tried using honey in my nose spray to kill whatever chronic growth was ailing me. Honey has natural anti-bacterial qualities, so I find it odd that bees are disappearing by the millions. Many believe it to be a bad sign of events to come.

Everything we need can be found naturally on Earth. Why are we seeking help from engineered chemicals? I watched Rocky make his own oil to regrow hair. He was feeling self-conscious and learned how to correct hair loss. He uses a combination of chili, olive and eucalyptus oils. I saw Rocky's hair grow back thick as a rug in just a few months.

We rely on doctors to educate us on our health issues, but they are unknowingly trained to lie to us. Most likely because of federal gag orders, I cannot get any medical explanation for the various bacterium, mold, and pathogens which were identified in my labs. If by chance my journey is not just coincidental nonsense, I may have received guidance how to cure myself despite the lack of medical treatment. If I can cure my own health with natural medicine, then I can help others cure their problems as well.

I want to end this session with a powerful and relevant quotation. I don't want you to think that this power is coming from me or my words. I often find His communication cleverly hidden within irony.

> And at that time shall Michael stand up, the great prince which standeth for the children of thy people and there

shall be a time of trouble, such as never was since there was a nation [even] to that same time: and at that time thy people shall be delivered, every one that shall be found written in the book.

–Revelations, Daniel 12:1

Paranormal Investigators

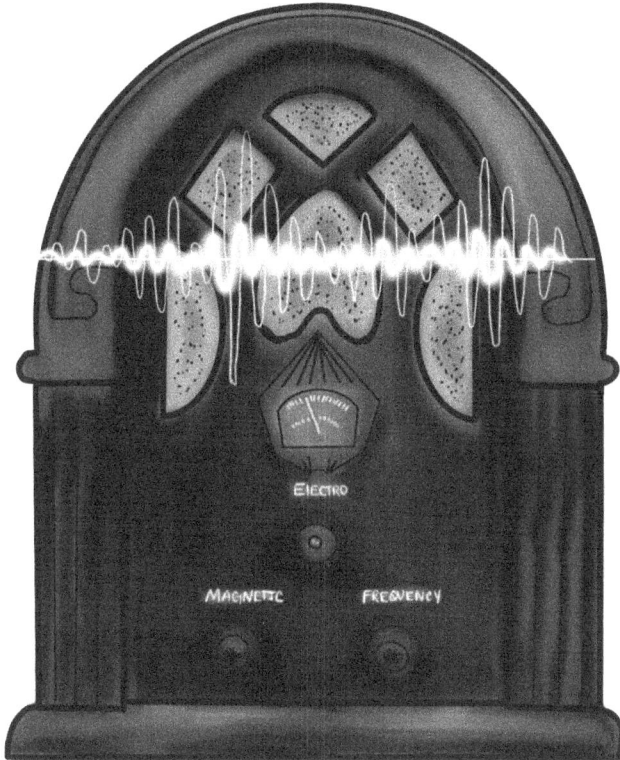

A good segue to this session would be to provide another glimpse of our current day in 2020. The Presidential election has come and gone, yet the US is still left in chaos with obvious signs and substantial evidence of voting fraud. The democratic party run by the Illuminati is using Biden and Harris as puppets. The Republican Party led by Trump and a secret force refuses to concede. The monsters I have previously mentioned are hiding within the Democratic Party using Trojan Horses, AI technology, false flag terrorism and engineered pandemics in a global effort to enslave humans.

The war of Good vs Evil has reached another pinnacle and the masses are blind to the fact that the prophecies from the Book of Revelations are upon us. If the people concede and allow the greatest mockery of the constitution to elect the Democratic party, Hell on Earth will slowly overtake us.

Because Eve bit the forbidden mushroom, humans will always be faced with a fungus. We need to regain control, though unfortunately a cleansing is necessary. Many forums call this cleansing "draining the swamp." My life ultimately depends on the public fighting to expose the corruption and the felonies committed by the Democratic party. If the Democrats win, the executions granted without due process will continue and I will not.

My role in this war is challenging. Lucifer has assassinated my character so badly that he has turned the world against me. I do not have any means to defend myself except through my writing. I cannot retaliate with self-defense because I will be the one incarcerated. I cannot shoot a gun or a bow or swing a sword. My only weapon is exposure, so I must write with blind faith as if the future of humanity depended on my words.

Rocky and I have not been able to build on our process. He has been assigned traveling duty for his job and even his overnight schedule makes it challenging to connect. I too started working part time and recently separated from Lori, who I still hold dear to my heart. The stress from my covert execution became too much for our relationship and the intentionally induced stress eroded whatever understanding Lori held for my situation. I believe the induced pain has become extreme because these demons are aware of my use of biblical medicine to combat the daily poisonings. I feel both obvious and subtle forces trying to prevent Rocky and I from finishing what we had started.

Since Rocky has been surrounded with paranormal activity all of his life, he has naturally met people with similar interests. He and a small group of enthusiasts began to conduct paranormal investigations. I joined them at a few locations and found instant satisfaction from observing their work.

One of the first paranormal investigations I observed was at a local legend in Hellertown, Pennsylvania. I suggested Hexenkopf Rock to the group since it has been investigated over the years and had its debut on a national TV series. Some have claimed to hear a woman's spirit speak and others have recorded a glowing red light there. At this point, I am looking for a deeper awareness in all possible forms of communication. Is there an obvious connection to link the paranormal world to life on Earth?

The group decided to investigate at dusk. In two separate vehicles, we meandered through the back hills of an old country town. Farmland and thick forest lined the roads with scattered farmhouses. We approached our destination called "Haunted Hill," and the crew began preparations. Rocky lit a bundle of sage and we took turns smudging each other. No one has ever provided a story or an explanation as to why this huge boulder and formation of massive rock enables paranormal communication. The group was hoping to get answers. Personally, I was hoping to reach a greater level of understanding. The jigsaw puzzle I am trying to piece together is multi-dimensional. I am still uncertain how Rocky's connection with the paranormal correlates to my own war with ancient monsters hiding within our government.

It was a cool summer night, and the sky was bright from a large waxing moon. The location was about fifty yards off the road in a thick wooded patch. I led the group of seven through the thicket until we approached the bottom of a massive hill comprised of boulders and rock. We climbed the daunting hill in pairs. Each pair helped the other secure a path. Large tree trunks seemed to move and tumble down on us as if we were in a game of Donkey Kong and thorny branches reached out to bite us through our clothing.

Finally, I reached the top and pulled two female members of the team up to the ledge. As the rest of the group reached the top, we fanned out to take in the view from Hexenkopf Rock. The view was enchanting and to be honest I didn't sense anything maleficent or dark. I checked Rocky for his reaction, which confirmed mine.

We took turns asking the spirit box various questions and recorded the session for review later. Although the group did not experience anything noteworthy, the location was about to provide some intense communication.

The group began its descent down the treacherous hill, weaving its way over and under logs. A few of us lost our coordinates on the way down, though eventually we reconvened where we had begun. We took one last look up at this so-called haunted legend, said our goodbyes, then came out of the woods and back to the vehicle. We thought we would be leaving unscathed.

Again, we smudged each other to protect our bodies from possession or physical harm. Smudging after an investigation helps prevent an entity from following someone who may be vulnerable. As I sat down in the driver's seat to start the car, I glanced down and noticed a few tiny black dots on my leg. I wasn't concerned until I saw them moving, and then I was horrified. There were dozens of tiny deer ticks on my pants leg. I got out of the car and saw hundreds, maybe thousands of ticks all over me. My shoes, socks, legs, sweats and shirt were all infested.

I shouted a warning to the group, and they too began to strip off clothing, fiercely wiping down their bodies. One poor girl with thick, beautiful hair screamed as we tried to pick them from her hair in the moonlight. Two girls were helping me wipe ticks off my back as a black pickup truck drove up and parked in the middle of the road to watch. Its windows were tinted and based on the make, model and color of the truck I knew they were government pawns sent to provoke a violent reaction from me. The entire group asked what the hell the truck was doing, though everyone was too preoccupied trying to get the blood sucking ticks off.

I am aware of the horrifying methods used by our government to eliminate targets, which is the reason I started to write in the first place. Not long ago, ticks were used as biological weapons. Engineered to carry diseases such as Lyme disease, millions of tics would be dropped onto designated areas. When the black truck eerily parked to observe us frantically swiping ticks off each other, my mind instantly recalled the lethal use of ticks, and my intuition told me the episode had to be an attack on me. Perhaps the desired response was for me to lash out at the truck,

The average person may think this idea is too far fetched and paranoid to believe. But try for a moment to see the world through my eyes. Understand what I have already survived and considering the many ways our government has already used lethal force to cover up secrets. Deer ticks could be considered a normal nature risk this time of year. But the entire group being covered in thousands of ticks seemed too unusual to be coincidental nonsense.

On the other hand, could this tick attack be the result of a paranormal force? Rocky had a dream where he was being attacked by a hive of demons controlled by one dominant demon. Could an unknown energy have been controlling the insects, much like the hive of demons that attacked Rocky? Is it just coincidental nonsense that I am writing to expose real life, blood-drinking monsters and we just got attacked by blood-drinking insects?

The creepy truck soon drove away and a few of us raised a finger as a parting gift while the rest packed our contaminated clothing into plastic bags. As soon as I got home, I checked my naked body for any lingering ticks. I noticed one on my stomach already burrowing into my skin. I yanked it out. Considering that I am legally being poisoned to death, I wonder if those ticks were carrying my cause of death. But then, considering I am blocked from getting legal and medical help, I may never know for sure.

This entire investigation had escaped my mind until I began compiling my thoughts for this session. I was never able to review the words captured by the spirit box. When reviewing video and audio clips, or even old vacation pictures, sometimes supernatural communication becomes more evident later. When I began to revisit memories of the night with Rocky, he explained that we did not leave that haunted hill alone.

I believe that some paranormal entities are fearful, even controlled by Rocky's power, and that's why Rocky doesn't fear possession or direct harm from them. I have become completely desensitized to fear and numb to mortality. I believe acceptance of death naturally defends against dark energy.

Earlier, I said that Lori had begun seeing shadows and experiencing unexplained phenomena in the apartment while home alone. Since I moved out, Lori witnessed a drastic increase in unusual events. From closet doors opening on their own to impression of an invisible being on the bed next to her, the phenomena have become frightening. I became instantly aware of a dark force when Abby, Lori's dog, died in bed one night while sleeping next to her. Abby was old, though I do not believe it was her natural time to pass. Much like the time Pedro was choked by the shadow standing on his chest, I am compelled to believe a similar energy suffocated Abby in her sleep.

For whatever the reason, Rocky and I seem to ward away this energy despite how much we provoke entities. That night on top of Hexenkopf Rock, I believe the group had been marked. The group did not have the same warding power as Rocky and I did. Something powerful had followed them home from the forest and the energy was strong enough to ignore the ritualistic defenses of smudging. Later, one of the couples on the team experienced violent disturbances in their apartment. One night a decorative sword seemed to pivot its handle against the wall, falling with a slashing motion and destroying a television below. Other members of the group complained of similar activity and even dealt with lingering ailments.

Did we provoke a dark energy that evening in the forest? Were the thousands of ticks a natural event, a paranormal phenomenon, or the result of a personal attack by the Illuminati? What I know is that the entire group, excluding Rocky and I, began to be haunted intensely. Lori became tormented more often in my absence and her dog mysteriously died.

I went into that forest with an inviting attitude. I provoked the energy more than anyone else because I want answers and I held zero fear. So why did the others feel the retaliation and not Rocky and me? Is a larger force, or perhaps a deeper power, trying to speak to us?

I believe the more I reach out to those other worlds, the better I become at hearing the unspoken languages. When we see a chair move across the room or a doll turn its head, we may assume the activity is from some pissed off spirit. I find this concept amusing because how many times do our current text messages get read with a different tone and get completely taken out of context?

A picture flying off the wall at you could provoke various explanations. Maybe someone on the other side can see our world and how close we are to being enslaved by monsters. Perhaps they are trying to get our attention and warn us by flinging pictures off the wall. Maybe a doll moving by itself is a deceased relative trying to spend time with the family. Perhaps the very same monsters enslaving the living have entrapped the dead. These monsters I am at war with may be trafficking souls in the spiritual world, just as monsters are trafficking people on Earth. Welcome to my war.

Sometime later, Rocky and 'Ana invited me to a spirit box session in her house—the house where the bread was mysteriously falling off the top shelf. Recall the shadow, the birdcage, and the three spirits who made it clear they still occupied the house? I was eager for a promising opportunity to have "in person" contact. The communication I received could both prepare me for war and secure my faith.

'Ana's shallow confidence had already been mocked with physical attacks. Rocky and I knew we might not have an accurate session because 'Ana was unprofessional and disorganized. So, we prepared well but held few expectations. As soon as I walked into the house, I sensed an uncomfortable pressure. It felt like someone had turned down the oxygen level in the house and every breath was heavy. I looked up toward the stairs and although it is hard to put into words, I felt the weight of heavy air falling on me.

Then, the real world allowed me to identify why so much negative energy was overtaking the home. The laws of attraction can help explain the situation. The house was in disorder. Several pit bulls were too much for the square footage of the house. A large, poorly maintained aquarium gave the room an algae odor.

A teenage daughter seemed to have demons within her already. Even without the dark energy, I would have felt uncomfortable in this house. I leaned into Rocky and quietly said, "I understand why 'Ana was strangled during one of her own sessions playing with a Ouija board." She claimed to be able to control, rebuke and identify demons, yet she cannot control her own environment. This is the type of mockery that feeds dark energy.

Rocky created a tone with his singing bowl. A chime or tone can be used to invite spirits into a particular session. The tone can also be used to identify where spirits are coming from and to help release trapped energy. Rocky and I sat at the dining room table.

While 'Ana and Rocky were setting up the table with spirit boxes, candles and various tools, I was listening to the slurred speech of 'Ana's husband. I could see the events he was describing as I have already dream walked through Rocky's memories. Pretending to listen to his drunken rambles about the events in the house, I was instead thinking of ways to obtain personal information from beyond our world. Piecing together his choppy, incomplete sentences, I realized that whatever messages received tonight during our investigation may provide answers.

I need a foundation of basic information to learn how to fight this biblical war. While I sat in a chair pretending to listen to 'Ana's husband, something told me to interrogate these spirits. I knew this was a unique situation to use the haunted house as a gateway.

We all sat down, and 'Ana began to communicate to the entity. We had constant interruptions from teenage kids getting up and down and knocking on the front door. The situation was a mockery to the entire practice, though I remained determined to get direct communication. As 'Ana and Rocky took turns asking questions, I wrote down the names, words and phrases recorded from the spirit boxes. Nothing stood out to me until a pattern finally became evident. Some words and phrases were being repeated three times. Once I recognized the pattern, I knew I was dealing with a demon.

Paranormal investigators sometimes see scratches etched in trees, walls and even on people. Markings of three lines is a mockery of the Holy Trinity—the Father, the Son, and the Holy Spirit. Once I saw the pattern of each name or word being recorded three times, I decided to get answers. I needed to provoke the demon so I could use it as a gatekeeper.

Although I was merely a guest during this session and I had no connection to the house, I boldly spoke up and intentionally provoked the room. With a condescending tone and attitude, I antagonized the demon. "Don't be scared. Show yourself."

I invited the entity to use me and my energy, giving the demon every means to communicate with me. Suddenly, the spirit box began to say vulgar words, each repeated three times. I wrote down the responses: Slut, slut, slut. Fuck you, fuck you, fuck you. Ass, ass, ass. Whore, whore, whore.

Of course, demons are going to communicate crudely. However, the words held meaning. Rocky believed the demon was mocking the mind of the teenage daughter who acted like she already had demons inside her. Since I was intentionally making myself vulnerable for communication purposes, I believe the words were more personal to me. Allow me to quickly summarize my role.

While suffering through intentional poisonings and mind-altering technology, I woke up and exposed human trafficking undertaken with the intention of sadistic pleasure, sacrifice and cannibalism consumption. Unfortunately, most of the poor souls being sold like a commodity are children. Along this journey with Rocky, I started to see and hear the world in four and possibly five dimensions. I assure you, many people around the world are beginning to see the world as I do.

A global conglomerate was contracted to discredit my suffering, attempting to cover up how millions of people were being tortured and murdered with this same fungus. This led to epic persecutions of targeted individuals including me, the goal of which is to humiliate and demoralize us by provoking our basic human instinct of self-defense and stimulating violent outbursts. Many targets around the world are being mutated into suicidal and homicidal maniacs. Character assassination discredits the target and propaganda fools perpetrators into participating in the torture and crucifixion of the targets. Does this program sound like a familiar Bible story?

There are millions of targets being tortured and crucified all around the world. Through my eyes, I see small, individual reenactments of the crucifixion of Jesus Christ that mock us all in plain sight.

Rocky and I left that haunted hill in Pennsylvania with little evidence but the group was followed home and tormented. Why do I not get attacked or threatened by the paranormal like many other people around Rocky? Why is it so hard for me to bring these entities into my light? Why is a powerful, global conglomerate having such a difficult time shutting me up or ending me? Now I am more empowered than ever before.

Sitting at the table, I began to demand a response from the demon. I egotistically said to the Demon, "Do you know who I am? Give me something."

Ana chimed in and asked the spirit box who was trying to communicate with the group. I didn't care about the identity of the demon—I wanted information from the other side.

I stared at a computer monitor showing a live stream of the adjoining room. This was the first time I had access to a demon on the other side and I wasn't about to waste the opportunity. So, I screamed at the demon in my thoughts. My face became red. I demanded over and over, "Give me something!" Then, Ana read out loud a name that appeared suddenly on the spirit box. Rocky and I looked at each other with understanding. The name was Abigail.

To be honest, with that name coming from a demon I had received all the information I needed that night. I excused myself from the table and walked out to sit on the front porch. The street was filled with neighborhood kids of all ages. Paid perpetrators were following their satellite GPS travel paths and racing down the street to provide stalking harassment. My war had just become clear. I may have just stumbled upon the entire purpose for our journey.

When I felt this project shift from paranormal to biblical, I allowed us to drift along without much direction until now because of the name Abigail. Let me explain.

The Illuminati is Lucifer's army. The Catholic Church was a Trojan Horse. The Illuminati held power within England and took their shot at enslaving the New World. Their arrogance got the better of the Elite, so the New World Order was stalled. Then, the Illuminati established roots in the Nazi party and used Hitler as a puppet. It grew into an incredible world threat. Once again, though, arrogance splintered their army, forcing the Illuminati to find a new Trojan Horse. Nazi scientists were well ahead of America on alien technology; therefore, America began to provide domicile and luxury accommodations to key Nazi players.

Here is a news flash—Hitler didn't kill himself after all.

During this time, we had incidents like the crash in Roswell, New Mexico, followed by the creation of Area 51. Weeks later, the CIA was created. Now what makes the Illuminati's Trojan Horse stand out like a sore thumb is that this global conglomerate was given the land by the CIA and grew roots into the industrial military complex. Funding was provided, laws were manipulated, and the empire was given permission to govern itself.

Here is another news flash—Walt Disney wasn't exactly frozen.

Ancient monsters have been practicing dark magic in combination with technology. They can transfer consciousness into another human mind or an artificial mind. Once again, I will throw the term out there—Nazi Necromancers.

Like the influence of the Catholic Church, this modern-day Trojan Horse has grown to a power that is incalculable. They own media, networks, military, political seats, Hollywood, and have deep roots into the very fabric of our society. As this empire has been making children adore and idolize their creations, they are raping, trafficking and consuming millions of children. I am not here to sugarcoat the harsh and disturbing reality. This empire, controlled by that ancient family, has been exposed for auctioning and trafficking children from an amusement ride. The constructed scene was clearly marked by the Freemasons, proving the Illuminati has contaminated many affiliations including military and governmental agencies.

Now that I see the world clearly, I recognize this entire corporation is a mockery. The entertainment they provide has hidden smut, mocking our reproduction organs and the life cycle itself. They are cleverly indoctrinating our children while mocking us with child trafficking and sex slaves in the movies they produce. While some families spend every vacation idolizing these icons, millions of children are being processed and sold for adrenochrome blood. Happy Place is luring you in with an end in mind—to enslave you.

This is the Antichrist.

When you use magic for evil or a maleficent intent, the laws of magic will come back around three-fold and smack the student back to reality. Perhaps my genetic susceptibility to that biblical fungus was my mark, or my wake-up call. Maybe the forces didn't stage my trip to a theme park in Florida that accepted a military contract to gaslight indoor mold as a bioweapon. Maybe a higher power needed me there, during a period where I was figuratively in hell. I crawled out of the fiery pits dragging Lucifer behind me.

If Hitler and Jeffery Epstein didn't kill themselves, then … are they still alive? Did they take the identity of another? Is Walt Disney walking and talking in another meat suit? If this ancient family is playing with dark magic, carrying out rituals to help Lucifer, then I must assume their own blood child was used as a sacrificial offering to the Dark Prince. Is Abigail the offspring of a human and an entity that is not of this world? Did Abigail herself give her womb to the Antichrist?

I do not have all the pieces needed to finish this puzzle, but my focus is now abundantly clear.

Could the events and experiences Daniel witnessed allow him to be a prophet of the Lord? Am I just a scribe? If Daniel were right and I somehow contain the bloodline of a Nephilim, could my visions and automatic writing be my purpose?

Rocky has helped me stay alive with love, knowledge and fasting. He introduced me to the paranormal world where I would ultimately speak to a demon.

I mentioned earlier that there are many worlds surrounding our own. Humanity is stuck in a three-dimensional state. People who are not empowered have a difficult time acknowledging the other worlds around us.

I wonder sometimes how many dimensions exist. My mind often gets stuck on the concept of energy from those other dimensions. I assume these other worlds communicate often, but without the right translator the messages are ignored or misunderstood. A perfect example was a message from Vrillon 1977. Vrillon told us outright that it was from another world. The entire broadcast disruption was shoved under the rug and its warning for humanity was soon forgotten.

How many other communications has the world received without most of us knowing the message? Are our leaders negotiating with these other worlds that will affect the entire human race and the future of humanity? When the large floating pyramid was spotted hovering over the Pentagon, did we surrender?

The state of our world is witnessing the Book of Daniel play out right before its eyes. The Democratic party and the puppet masters are trembling with fear. They are desperately trying to enslave the masses with witchcraft and sorcery before the world learns of their mass genocide. For as long as these monsters have been on this Earth, millions of children have been ritualistically raped, tortured and drained of their blood. These monsters who are now running our government are fulfilling Lucifer's vision of Hell on Earth.

I see things which I am just not supposed to see. I suppose the years of pain and torture could have helped open my mind. Fasting and praying with mug-wart, frankincense and myrrh as helped open up my spirituality. I have been practicing dream walking and astral projection. Perhaps I have unknowingly tapped into some hidden potential. Once, while in a daydream, I saw a magnificent room. On one wall was a large, gold-framed painting of the iconic amusement park I call Happy Place. In my vision I saw the hinged painting swung open to reveal a large wall safe. In the wall safe, I saw a dozen glass jars containing what appeared to be dark blood. In my dream walk, this estate belonged to Abigail.

In a different session of this dream walking or perhaps astral projection I found myself traveling through hallways. Beneath this amusement park created on CIA-granted land, miles and miles of corridors mysteriously weaved into an entire underground city extending in layers deep into the earth. Each layer became more disturbing and required special access. I saw laboratories filled with geneticists. Deeper, I saw rooms where masked figures were raping children. Deeper yet I felt the presence of beings, and although they were invisible, I knew they were astonished to see me.

In a separate vision, I saw political figures sitting in a capsule like one in an airplane. I could tell this was not a plane, though, because the windows looked out into the ocean. I saw a handful of people in a submarine traveling to an underwater base off the shore of Epstein's Island. (I should tell you that human remains are being uncovered from this infamous Pedovore Island.)

I do not know why I have these visions or daydreams, though I do believe them to hold truths. Is my purpose to simply write my thoughts? George Washington warned that the Illuminati had infiltrated the Freemasons and possessed a bad intention for America. Two hundred years later, our own government allowed the Freemasons to construct a scene for an amusement ride specifically meant to traffic children. The Freemasons arrogantly branded the scene with their infamous logo.

So, if we didn't listen to George Washington's written warning, who the Hell is going to listen to mine? Our own government murdered President JFK so the Illuminati wouldn't have any interference with its vision of Hell on Earth. If they killed the President of the United States and got away with it, what can I possibly do to stop my own crucifixion, not to mention casting Lucifer back to Hell?

I pray, "Holy Father, how do I begin? Where do I start? If Lucifer is my purpose, you must know he has built himself an empire backed by a worldwide militia. With blind faith and pure devotion, I am charging. Give me direction!"

In my dream, this is the answer to my prayer.

My Son,

You have something that George Washington didn't have at the time. You hold a unique situation that would have prevented John F. Kennedy from being blindsided. You have a stage. Our heroes of the past did not have the technology to warn and influence the mass population for the greater good. Your stage has grown so large, your messages are instantly reaching people on other continents. The demons who are broadcasting your life, selling the live streaming of your "Slow Kill," are also creating a video imprint … providing eyewitnesses to your torture and murder. If you were shot and killed, a vast audience tuning into your show will see it all documented in real time. Therefore, these demons try to covertly stage accidents and poisonings because everything they do is being recorded, which means everything you say and write is being collected, stored and analyzed.

This is your purpose.

I will show you all the evil hiding on Earth so you can identify and describe it, yet know that understanding this knowledge will bring inhumane pain. No matter how much pain, suffering and torment you may endure, know that I am with you. Also, trust that my light is spreading through you. You will continue for I need you to shine.

Know Thy Enemy

I have learned a great deal from watching both fictional and nonfictional entertainment. Many screenplays and real-life paranormal investigators claim that the first step in fighting monsters is learning what you're up against. I know Lucifer walks the Earth. I believe his child is desperately trying to finish the last few spells necessary to cast a darkness over the land, bringing about Hell on Earth. I also hold faith we are going to stop the Apocalypse and save the world.

I must now present the testimony from an eyewitness to the horror of Happy Place. I believe this poor man's story was sent to me by a higher power. As you read through this real-life horror story, try to project yourself into the scene allowing the words to come to life. I need you to know the enemy and see the enemy as I do. The dark and disturbing truths are right in front of us all, though the devil's persuasion is clever. The Trojan Horse is luring children and families into a fantasy world while mocking us with the horrors hidden in plain sight. It is about time all of you learn how the Devil operates. You may join me on my biblical task to take Lucifer back to Hell, or you can choose to sit back and watch me. Trust, if you are put in my way to divert my effort, I will go through you.

Good morning! I am writing this on my phone, so please have patience with any grammatical or formatting errors. This post got removed originally, and I messaged the mods. They said they have no idea how it happened, but I've been finding small silhouettes of a mouse outside of my house. Here's the repost, and an update is in the works.

To start off with, I now reside in a completely different state after leaving my job with the Happy Place Resort in Asto Luego, Florida. I used to be what one other Redditor described as a "suit"; I am one of the guys that walks around the park in plain sight yet hidden to the public. I am part of the elite group of black-polo-sporting undercover security officers that specialize in worse things than shoplifters and unruly park guests. You see, as stated prior to this post on /r/nosleep, if you are at Happy Place and you see more than a few guys in one place wearing black polos, then you are most likely in danger and you should leave the area immediately. The sad part is, we are so good at blending in with the woodwork that you wouldn't even notice us. Anyway, let me cut to the chase here. I have seen some weird things at Happy Place during my time. These "anomalies" that everyone speaks of, well, they are true, but the least of our concerns. See, the thing is, when you take hundreds of thousands of people and cram them into a relatively small space, weird shit is going to happen. We have had kids, even adults, get lost in the park and cryptozoological sightings, alien sightings, ghost sightings, and just generally unexplainable things happen all the time.

I was a senior special security officer during the height of my time there and got called for some dark shit. Many of you think we, as in the security detail I was in, were covering up for Happy Corp., but in our true nature, we were damage control and were kept out of the loop on things and were trained not to question but to diffuse. There was one thing, though, that, to this day, still bothers me. A cast member called us on the Nextel to report that a group of four children had gone missing on the Land. Of course, I thought, another one of those anomalies. For those of you who don't know the eerily calming nature ride called Living with the Land, it is in the Land and the Sea pavilion over by Soarin'. The odd thing about this report is that we have never received one of these complaints before, and of course, we are issued cover-up stories to tell cast members or guests to calm them down. My colleague calmly came up with a story and explained that the kids were part of an educational program and they exited the boat with a guide and were escorted into the botany lab that exists on the ride. I told her not to ask any questions or talk about the incident as to not spread "false rumors" and had my colleague escort her to a nearby security office to have her sign some forms. My human nature took over, and I got curious and entered the ride on the next boat alone.

Living with the Land is boring and not particularly popular, so I can understand how the kids would be on the boat alone and how I could get on the boat by myself. I noticed absolutely nothing until I came to the part of the ride that has the prairie farmhouse. It looks like a faux house, but something about it just never sat right with me. As I have done hundreds of times before on rides, I jumped off the boat and onto the scene where the house is. I noticed something funny, though. There were no pressure mats, and the boat went away, allotting about a good thirty seconds before the next boat got to the scene. I have never seen a ride with no pressure mats to detect if anyone disembarks the ride.

So quick recap: Kids disappeared on ride, I showed up and fed the cast member who reported it some story about how they disembarked midride and were on a tour of the lab and for her not to question it. A colleague of mine took her away to debrief. I contacted the new cast member operating the ride and told him to put some space between the next boat as I was looking for a lost wedding ring. Bull, I know, but so what?

I slowly started to walk up to the faux house. Climbing the steps up to the porch, I noticed a small emblem on the left window. It was a small square and compass symbol. Interesting that a Masonic symbol was hidden here. I figured whoever built the ride was a Freemason and brushed it off. I looked in the windows of the house, and it was nothing but curtains with black plywood behind them. I thought that there was nothing to see here, but still, something inside me decided that wasn't good enough. The front door glided open to a bright room with a black-and-white checkerboard floor. There was a marble altar-like table on the opposite end of the room, with a weird, throne-like chair built into the front of it and a gold cup on the tabletop. The only other thing that was noticeable was a heavy wooden door on the other end of the room that was locked; there were no windows or anything else. I thought it was weird because I was always under the impression that this house was fake. Human nature took over again, and against my better judgment,

I tried the door in the room, but I was relieved that it was locked. I tried my keys, but none of them worked. Here's the thing: At Happy Place, we use a lock system called Best. This had interchangeable cores that have assigned numbers and/or letters. This is so we can issue keys only to certain areas. I have the general master key, which essentially is the real key to the kingdom. Interesting thing about this lock was that my master didn't open it. I looked closer, and it was a Best Lock, but the inscription said "CC." on it, which I've never seen before. Since the door wasn't open, I decided to just leave. On my way, out I noticed in the floor there was a fast pass printed out for Soarin'. I picked it up and pocketed it; it's amazing how trash works its way into odd places. I'm going to figure out where these kids went.

I rode the boat back out to the platform and went back to the Epcot security office to play back some footage from the DVR. It took me a while, but I zeroed in on the period where the kids entered the Land and Sea Pavilion and followed them. There were four kids total, three girls and one boy. The girl's actions were almost robotic, and it sent a chill up my spine. They walked in a straight line through the pavilion, but what scared me was, there was a man with them escorting them through the place. I paused and looked closer when I realized the man was wearing black polo and khakis, the same thing I was wearing. Holy shit! I even recognized him—it was one of my colleagues.

Allen is the guy that was at the scene before I got there, the same guy who fed the cast member at the control podium the bullshit about the kids going on a tour. I thought maybe he did send them on the tour of the botanical lab and lost track of them, until I hit Play on the film. The boy was not walking in line, and I could tell he was giving Allen problems; he kept venturing away and getting distracted by various things in the Pavilion. The benefit of the doubt I gave Allen subsided when I saw the kid go press

the button for the fast pass on Soarin' and take the paper
fast pass almost like a prize. Allen then tugged him away
and stood back and observed as the kids walked to Living
with the Land. I saw them get on the boat. I saw them
through the storm scene, through the rain forest scene,
then through the desert scene. After the desert, I lost the
boat on camera. The ride stopped momentarily; you could
see it on the other scenes. And once it resumed, I saw the
boat again in the scene with the pictures of farmers. The
boat was empty. I also saw freakin' Allen looking down off
the observation deck, which explains how he responded
so quickly. I switched the cameras back to live view and
left that area. I haven't been exactly honest with you thus
far. I know a lot of the things that Happy Place does and
things that we respond to that a regular security officer
wouldn't deal with. I have seen them experiment on so
many things, such as eugenics, pharmaceutical engineering, even experimenting with gas. Have you ever noticed
that on both Spaceship Earth and the Monorail, you get
a strange, calm feeling on those rides? Well, they are
pumping low doses of laughing gas in those areas. Ever
heard of Room 0? They were wearing gas masks for a
reason. Ever hear of Gascots? Well, that's not important
right now. I would encourage you to research it. I never
thought that what we did was okay by containing these
dark secrets, but it paid well. I have seen them quickly
inject some experimental drug on guests and throw them
back out there. Our job was to monitor and contain them
if things went haywire. I know that I am the bad guy, but
this wasn't normal. This wasn't procedural.

First thing I did was go over to the room where we keep
the keys. I looked through the logbooks for the core
labeled "CC." I found it, but it had no zone or specific
location issued to the core, and the number of copies was
marked as 1. This key was in our system, but my master
key didn't open it. I grabbed the "core key" and a few
zone 1 cores. The core key is a specific key that, when

inserted into the lock, will remove the core so it can be replaced with another. I put this in my pocket and made a beeline for the Land and Sea Pavilion. I may be paranoid, but I swear I saw Allen following me in the shadows.

I got to the ride and got to the house and back in the front door to the Masonic room and locked the front door as I entered. I inserted the core key into the lock on the wooden door, removed the core, and inserted the zone 1 core into the lock. Now, my master key will open the door, and boy did it. The door glided open. It was heavy and steel on the other side of the wood face. There was a red-velvet-carpeted staircase leading down to some kind of utilidor, but we are in EpcoT. What the hell. There is one small utilidor in EpcotT, but it doesn't go this deep. I descended the stairs and walked down the red-carpeted hallway to these two double doors. Behind these doors was my answer and the truth as to what happened to these kids. Through these doors was the darkest side of Happy Place, a side of Happy Place that even I couldn't believe. Would Walt be in favor of this? Or was this one of Eisner's little idea of making more money off his guests?

Behind these doors was an empty, dimly lit room with a small circular platform in the center. The carpet was the same lush red velvet carpet from the hallway. There were six leather armchairs around the circular platform, all with telephones and card readers on the table next to the chair. Inside I knew what was going on. I knew what was happening here. This is one thing I will not cover up for the Happy Corp. I stood there in disbelief and horror and noticed a small door toward the back of the room. I went over and popped out the "CC" core, put it in my pocket, and put in a zone 1 core. I heard someone clear their throat from the front of the room. It was Allen. He had an annoyed look on his face and held a gun trained at me. I slowly propped the door open on the latch and turned to face him.

"You never should have come here," he said to me when he was stepping toward me.

"So, this is what you and your scumbag friends have resorted to? We did some pretty fucked-up shit, Allen, but this is a new low for you and your disgusting friends." I had my hand at my side and blocked the view of me slipping the zone 1 core out of the handle and into my pocket.

"It's not going to matter, because no one is going to find out."

He raised the gun, and like something out of an action movie, I ripped the door open as he pulled the trigger and a bullet hit the door. I jumped backward through the doorway and shut it behind me. That asshole was stuck because I had both cores in my pocket, so there was no way he could open the door. He started shooting the door, and I moved forward. I walked down a hallway with these small cell-like rooms lining the hall, and inside were those playschool chairs and a few toys. I checked every one of them, and they were all empty. I got to the end of the hall, and there was this huge vault-like metal door. I popped the last zone 1 core into the door to replace the "CC" core and pulled the steel door open to be hit in the face with sunlight. I was outside on some side utility road off premises of epcoT. The road led away. I was too late; they were already gone for good.

I called the police, but they never came. I called the FBI, but they never took me seriously. Hell, I even called the CIA, but they said they didn't deal with domestic issues like that and referred me back to the FBI. I showed up at the Orange County Police Department HQ, and they took a report, but I heard something fall in the trash when I was leaving. Happy Place is good at what they do: they are good at keeping secrets, and they are good at controlling any outside force that attempts to bring their secrets to light. I am lucky I saw the sunlight again and am lucky to have had time to leave the state before they got to me. If you go there, please keep your kids close. Watch out for the guys in the black polos. They may be monitoring you; they may be responding to something that will put you in danger. As far as I know, they aren't the ones that pick out the merchandise. I don't even know who does that.

The second story of the house is seemingly normal, but I don't know how they access it. You'll also notice that there is an observation deck; this area was undergoing "maintenance" at that time. It was closed off to guests, but CCTV footage revealed nothing was happening in that area. The camera points back onto the observation area and not at the house. There are no cameras in that portion of the ride.

I have nothing further to say.

Session XV

KnockKnock Enoch

This journey with Daniel has led us to a historical and revolutionary time in history. We began this project with no true end in mind. I had felt the need to bring many different pieces together to complete a multidimensional jigsaw puzzle. I knew Daniel's experiences and his gifts must hold a deeper meaning. Daniel personally introduced me to the paranormal world and with his support, prolonged my life. More importantly, he kept me fighting.

During this adventure, I have mysteriously become aware of entities hiding adjacent to our realm along with seeing the true faces of monsters in our own world. My new found perceptions could be the result of cleansing my pineal gland. These visions may be from meditation using mug-wart and other biblical medicines. Perhaps the pain and suffering has opened doors to my mind. More likely than not, I believe the combination has empowered my body, mind and spirit. For what purpose? I refuse to allow my visions to be documented, though nothing can be done to stop the Hell on Earth that I am cursed to envision. Nostradamus documented two steel birds destroying massive towers, yet nothing was done to stop them.

But I refuse to allow history to repeat itself. My only weapon is a pen, and I was told to continue. So, continue with faith I shall.

Since this journey naturally shifted from paranormal to biblical, I must identify the hidden synergy that is being communicated. The world adjacent to our own has allowed me to speak to a demon, providing me with confirming direction. We are obviously connected, though we are somehow cut off from seeing these other dimensions all around us. Allow me to document another update to the current state of our world which will help clarify these other dimensions.

We are at war. Some may call it Civil War; others may call it World War. I call it Revelations. No matter the name, As it is written, It must be so. January 10th, 2021, the Vatican experienced an intentional blackout and was seized shortly after the POTUS signed the Insurrection Act of 1807. Many rumors are spread with false news; however, I know the Great Awakening is upon us. The secret force known as Q is trying to prevent the enslavement of humanity, and the effort is being whispered through the channels with little information or recognition. Monsters will be rounded up in herds and taken to FEMA camps all around the world. Mass pedovorism will be exposed on a global scale. These shocking religious, political, and social icons will reveal their true identities along with every detail pertaining to their intimate dedication to the Illuminati. I will not rest until the masks are removed and true faces are revealed.

We are living biblical times, and I feel a burning passion to comprehend all the communication. This task is challenging considering that the communication is coming from various sources and different worlds. If the Roman Catholic Church goes down for being the Trojan Horse for ancient monsters, then what is the communication for humanity? Daniel was once told to find answers written in the book. I will listen to that communication and proceed to the Book of Enoch.

Before I dive into another dream walk, I feel I must provide an explanation as to why the Book of Enoch will guide us to a transition from this journey to the next. In addition to the constant paranormal interaction, Daniel also had a UFO encounter. Like so many other witnesses, he saw a hovering light. Rocky couldn't explain the feeling too well, though I think he felt a connection to this light, as if it were focusing on him. Then, the light beamed out of sight. I never studied documents and history regarding the conspiracy around aliens until Rocky wanted me to watch the documentary called "Unacknowledged." The corruption and secrecy unveiled in it became tangled in my mind and created an itch that I couldn't scratch. Seeking a satisfactory explanation seemed to become more important to me then stopping my own legal execution I am still facing today.

From the thousands of pages and various versions, the Book of Enoch is one of the lesser books studied. It is organized into five parts containing over ninety texts—Book of Watchers, Book of Parables, Book of Luminaries, The Dream Visions, and The Epistle of Enoch.

Considering that we are approaching the dawn of truth, we must come together as a human race and accept we have never been alone on this Earth. In fact, we must accept that our God is much different than we had originally imagined. Make no mistake, though, we still must follow the true light. We must come to grasp the reality that humanity was, in fact, engineered. Perhaps we were created to work the land, mining precious metals from the Earth for our creators. Whatever the case, somewhere along the journey, life found a way. Therefore, I hold the concept of free will in high regard. We were created in His image.

If we were created by another advanced life form, then I can also acknowledge other, more sinister life forms are trying to enslave humanity. This is why the Book of Enoch is relevant to me. I could spend a lifetime studying these stories, though my time is limited. Therefore, I must use what I am given without much education. The peculiar thing about the Enoch writings is that other books of the Bible do not mention much about Enoch. In fact, the book of Genesis only devotes a few passages to this older Testament.

Genesis 5:24 Enoch walked with God; then he was no
more, because God took him.

I am not educated or accredited, though somehow these words speak to me differently. Today, we would call this encounter with God an abduction. If you ever played the game "Whisper Down the Alley" in grade school, you would understand how messages become distorted with each new person who shares the message. Since translation becomes inevitably distorted over thousands of years with countless story tellers, the people refer to Enoch disappearing as "God took him."

The fact that our ancient ancestors came in direct contact with many different alien species worries me because of their absence today. The mass population doesn't interact with these beings at all, at least not knowingly. So why such the secrecy now? I have a feeling many of these shadow entities already ascribed may be alien and not paranormal at all. Perhaps they are beings colliding with our world, though because they are fourth and fifth dimensional, we can only see them as shadows. I'm not taking anything away from Casper our friendly ghost, but as far as shadow entities are concerned, I don't think they are in the ghost category.

The little bits and pieces I know about the Book of Enoch tell me humanity is in danger of being enslaved by an ancient life form. These creatures have been toying with us since the beginning of humankind and each time they come close to overthrowing us, their arrogance causes them to make mistakes and give heroes like George Washington, John F. Kennedy and Trump an opportunity to sustain our way of life. We are seeing another epic example of their arrogance today, and I assure you, the masks will be removed and these pedovors will be exposed.

Genesis 6 1 - 4 Divine beings having sex with humans.

Before Noah's flood, it was written that divine beings came to Earth to have sex with women. The women then gave birth to

Nephilim, (Bne Elohim) Warriors of God and warriors renowned. These children were known as "Mighty men that were of old."

Humanity must begin to accept that angels are not full of feathers and peace. Humans gave them wings because of their ability to fly down from the sky, which is always depicted as heaven. I don't want to start a religious war, but our so-called angels are really aliens. Some are here to watch over us. Others are here to enslave us.

The Book of Watchers teaches about an entire society of fallen angels led by Chief Samyaza. This fallen angel came to wreak havoc on Earth and took a third of the other angels with him. They began to teach weaponry, sorcery and astrology to humankind persuading us to use the powers for destruction and evil. I struggle to understand the giants. The children of these fallen angels were also Nephilim, and these giants began to kill man, devouring all beasts and drinking their blood.

I cannot help but compare the ritualistic sacrifices and consumption of human blood today by the Illuminati to the story of giants eating people and drinking blood. I believe there are ancient life forms that have been playing with our genetics. It is possible they were able to genetically alter the fifty-foot giants down to six-foot human lookalikes. Enormous skeletal remains are being unearthed today.

Were these cannibalistic giants genetically altered to blend in with humanity? Why were we never taught about these giants, and why the hell did they start eating people? What if the giants were the good guys and their true character was assassinated? Maybe the Giants were supposed to protect the land from the blood drinking monsters.

I am exposing an ancient family of creatures for drinking blood and trafficking children. I can't even speak to my own daughter because they labelled me a pedophile with their technology and sorcery. So, I know damn well Lucifer and his demons will use evil tactics to cover up truths. If a few of these watchers came to earth to wreak havoc, perhaps a third of these so-called angels were fooled by Lucifer and joined him on his quest to bring Hell on Earth.

As written in the Book of Enoch, God sent four Archangels. Gabriel was sent to destroy the Nephilim. "Go Gabriel, to the bastards, to the half breeds, to the sons of miscegenation and destroy the sons of the Watchers from among the sons of men."

Another Archangel was sent to warn Noah of the flood, and Enoch was sent to tell these watchers that they will be destroyed. Then, the God sends Archangel Michael to kill the King of the Watchers, Samyaza.

Perhaps this session will be the beginning of an entirely new adventure. For now, I need to discover how it relates to our current journey.

I am being crucified by the Illuminati in a battle for my soul. Most targeted individuals break down after a few years of torture and take their own lives or the life of one of their tormentors. Unfortunately, this sinful act leads to the damnation of their soul. I believe these entities masquerading as the Illuminati take pleasure in mocking us. In fact, I believe all evil and murder on this Earth since the beginning of man has been the result of Samyaza and his fallen watchers having fun.

After eight years of excruciating torture and emotional torment, I can still love and be loved. I am still free and alive to inspire others despite the horrific agony. There must be a reason for my loving, sustaining endurance.

I know I am no giant and I do not desire human flesh. Is it possible though, that my genetic mutation to a biblical fungus is a sign that a more advanced life form was playing with genetics, and that my susceptibility is a glitch in their engineering? Oddly enough, it was after Rocky noticed I was born with two toes on each foot webbed together that he claimed I had the blood of a Nephilim. To be quite honest, I have a few genetic defects that raise my curiosity.

I must look deeper yet. My ex-wife was sold as a child by her father for his initiation into the satanic Illuminati. I used to refer to her as the demon seed. Nothing in my life is a coincidence. The Illuminati planted their demon seed into my wife Gena and she has become their child. Twenty years later, I had a child with this woman. What does this mean for my daughter?

I know the Illuminati will protect my mob boss father-in-law and the child he sold to be raped, therefore I will be the one wrongly crucified. If I have the bloodline of a Nephilim, my daughter does as well. If my daughter was born from a mother who was sold to the Illuminati, what does this make my daughter? Could she be the savior? What will come of her own career and focus? When my daughter reads of the torture and heinous abuses her father had to endure, will she follow in my footsteps and help expose Lucifer and his army of Illuminati?

The giants or Nephilim were said to wreak havoc on Earth. When my life was systematically and intentionally destroyed, I too created havoc on Earth. I was angry, confused, and betrayed by those who were supposed to be family. The constant, covert espionage put scapegoat after scapegoat in my path, and each one has fallen over time. Despite the havoc created through attempts to discredit and silence me, I am still free and alive to use the only weapon my Holy Father gave me, and with each word I write I am slashing Lucifer down.

So, if the Book of Enoch is giving us signs that our entire existence is a lot easier to comprehend than our philosophers imagined, then why all the secrecy? If our ancient ancestors interacted with various species of alien life, why don't we get the same attention today. Or do we?

Ever since foo fighters were spotted hovering in our skies, man has tried to shoot them down. The crash of Roswell might not have been an accidental crash. Do you think this more advanced technology would crash on its own? So, if our so-called watchers were shot down because Lucifer and his fallen angels were coercing us to do so, this could be the reason we are seeing Revelations today.

These fallen angels taught man witchcraft and sorcery and gave them technology they would have never been able to discover in their own lifetime. Lucifer is clever, and he has been building the armies of the Illuminati for a long time. Believe me or not, many of our leaders today are warriors of Lucifer's army and have used the teachings of technology, witchcraft and sorcery to help bring Hell on Earth.

When Bill Gates meets with the CIA to pitch a vaccine that will genetically alter human spirituality, I am forced to see the true faces of these fallen angels. When Hitler orders the torture and execution of huge numbers of people, I am forced to see the true faces of these fallen angels. When Walt Disney creates an empire that begins to rape, traffic and consume children right on their CIA-granted land, I see the true faces of these fallen angels. I need you to see the false light being cast across the land.

If the Vatican, along with the Roman Catholic Church, gets exposed for being the largest Trojan Horse in history, is Disney next? How can we allow an empire to govern itself when we know they will continue to rape, traffic, and consume millions of children?

Is this my purpose? Is this the reason why I received the communication to "continue?" To know thy enemy is to see thy enemy. I see their true faces impersonating our own. How can I get others to see their demon faces as I see them?

The pain these last few days has been remarkable, and the amount of harassing street theater is a clear sign of their desperation. I have no doubt that the poisoning will prematurely end my life. But my Holy Father told me they will not take my soul. All I must do is die without retaliation and my soul lives on. Perhaps that is another way for me to continue. Many will watch me die, though it will not be the snuff film originally promised by these demons.

The Book of Daniel discusses the Archangel Michael as well, although it is Lucifer whom he casts down to Hell. Is this discrepancy an example of "Whisper Down the Alley?" If I am going to get you to reevaluate your concept of a higher power, I believe we all need to revisit the concept of Heaven and Hell as well. If Nostradamus described two planes crashing into towers as steel birds, then how do you think our ancient ancestors are going to describe the beings they saw come down from the sky?

These various gods and mythological creatures that people have worshipped for eons were nothing more than various types of alien life. So where are they now? Where did all these species run off to? Did they all go back to another galaxy, or did they learn how to live among us … perhaps *as us*?

Cohabitation sounds fine until you find out your next-door neighbor has been eating all the neighborhood kids. I don't mean this sarcastically. This is the alarming reality hidden right before our eyes.

I believe these shapeshifting cohabitants have spent the last two hundred odd years preparing for an enslavement. When the colonies broke free from England, we were supposed to be set up as a Republic. It turns out, the country was set up much like a corporation and the entire meaning of independence was an illusion. Bottom line, if you have a social security number and have not gone through the process of becoming a sovereign citizen, you are considered a corporation. You are basically property owned by a larger entity. Scary thought, I know. The use of debt is being used as a legally binding contract to enslave the country.

I have written a few times already about this vision of Hell on Earth. If these beings, which were documented in our scriptures, came down from space and not heaven, this affects my perception of Hell. If Heaven can be used as an enchanting fairy tale to explain where these beings come from, then where is the real Hell located— the Hell that we have been brainwashed to imagine as full of fire and brimstone?

If Aliens are all around us, then think of all the places on this Earth where they can be hiding. I mentioned how an enormous crystal pyramid is sitting on the bottom of the ocean in the middle of the Bermuda Triangle. Trust me, our military has known about that large pyramid for a long time. The reason our military does not want to provide natural gas to Asia is because it would require building a natural gas station along with underground gas lines on the west coast. They don't want to disturb the gigantic alien bases already residing there.

What if our perceptions of Hell come from descriptions from the center of the Earth? If you were an intelligent species planning your invasion of humanity, where would you hide? If the original watchers were here to make sure Samyaza didn't harm humanity, building an army below ground would provide the cover to remain hidden. Learning how to impersonate a human over time would allow covert cohabitation. Later, having our own military shoot the watchers down could end the watching altogether, allowing an evil to spread like a fungus.

In the Book of Enoch, the king of the watchers Samyaza came to Earth and began to lust for our women. Due to his evil intent, God sent Archangel Michael to kill Samyaza. But maybe Michael could not kill Samyaza. Maybe the king of watchers was fearful of Michael and hid in the deepness of Earth, providing a story line for the later scriptures which created the perception of Lucifer being cast down to Hell.

These pieces of a puzzle are now floating in space all around me, so indulge me for a minute. It was said that Samyaza was lustful for the women on Earth. Later it was written that Lucifer resented humanity and rebelled against God.

Allow me to bring you back to our current war of good vs evil. The Illuminati is mocking us in plain sight. I see modern day Trojan Horses creating a mockery of child trafficking, sex slaves, pornography and sorcery, all while casting the masses into a dream world. The 1940 movie *Pinocchio* was a cartoon clearly created to mock children being kidnapped and sold as a commodity. It was not coincidental nonsense that Walmart, through its success, eliminated mom and pop convenient stores. Next time you look at an Amazon Prime truck, try to see what I see. You may see a smile with an arrow at the end. I see a male penis mocking humanity in plain sight.

Allow me to psychoanalyze Samyaza. If I am the chosen one sent to cast Lucifer back to the center of the Earth, this may be why he has used his military goons to legally elect me for execution, once again mocking man. Is this why I have been slandered as a sex offender, a pedophile, and someone who suffers from an Oedipus complex? Is this why Abigail Disney is funding thousands of women to harass me into killing myself or someone else? Is this why Abigail Disney invited my wife and child down to Disney to coerce their involvement in my torture and execution? Samyaza is jealous and envious of man. The king of the watchers resents the way I look and the love I both receive and give.

When these fallen angels came to Earth and began having sex with women and children, they were mocking humanity. I believe that is when human blood began to be consumed. Women and children fought and tried to resist the hideous creatures; however, these rape victims gave birth to hybrids. The reason these entities started impersonating humans is because humans sexually rejected them. (Beauty and the Beast) Today, when Disney conducts their nightly costume orgies and satanic rituals, they wear masks to hide the true faces of some of the participants. These entities want to enjoy the ritual without a bio engineered plasma meat suit. And yes, over time, more and more hybrids are reproducing with humans, creating an intergalactic family tree.

The sexual mockery is blatantly obvious. From Hollywood to cartoons, children are being brainwashed with sex and smut, yet I am the one being tortured and crucified by women for being a domestic terrorist. Can you see the irony? Looking back at our history, every act of terrorism and war is the result of these idiots having fun with us.

I like to quote the line, "If you were aliens trying to take over the world, would you do it Independence Day style or would you sneak in through the back door." We have been mocked since the beginning of time, and with each decade, the Illuminati has staged wars, terrorism, pandemics and an overall evil, slowly breeding humanity away while enslaving the rest. Perhaps my writing is simply a therapeutic release, but the entire point of this journey is to get us all to start listening. The true light of God is all around us and we do have good angels watching over us. All we must do is listen and use our free will to act with decency, care and love.

If you are getting paid to torture, harm, and kill innocent people, all while knowing the orders are coming from pedophiles and pedovores, you are the problem. The solution is to remove all entities, including human ones, who have both participated in and allowed the rape, torture and consumption of millions of children since the beginning of humankind. This could be a third of the population, and I do enjoy His irony. There was a global plot known as Agenda 21 to decrease the world population by one-third. Perhaps the irony also carries His wrath.

Save The World

You will be restructured in a wholesome fashion. Every square inch of your CIA-granted land, both public and private, will be searched and investigated. You will cease and desist all military and shadow government contracts. You will no longer have the privilege of governing yourselves. You will admit and relinquish every asset, every estate, every account, every corporation, every entity, all technological projects, and every political seat you used to enslave the world up to this point. You will lose 51 percent of the entire empire removing you from control to ensure you are indeed, restructured in a wholesome fashion.

You will publicly apologize for your involvement with Nazi torture and human experimentation. You will apologize for arrogantly breaking humanitarian codes of ethics regarding eugenics, vaccines, and experimental pharmaceuticals. You will admit and apologize for mocking humanity and brainwashing our children with sex, smut and evil hidden within your entertainment.

Your entire existence revolving around pedovorism, which creates a Hell on Earth, will be exposed on a global scale. Your entire ancient family and blood line, no matter how much money and power they may hold, will be rounded up and held accountable for their crimes against humanity.

Then, Samyaza, you will accept my mercy. You will crawl back under that rock from which you came and return to the center of Earth. If you choose to stay and fight me, I will destroy you once and for all.

Thy name is Michael.
As it is written, it must be so.

Acknowledgements

From being a Targeted Individual and enduring the isolating character assassinations that go with it, I've learned that the people left standing by me are the ones who truly matter.

I want to give special thanks to my editor and designer Gary Lindberg. I believe people come into your life with a coincidental magic, and Gary's sincerity and professionalism is inspiring. I am grateful for both Gary and publisher Ian Graham Leask for their willingness to accompany me on this journey.

To my beloved mother and father, thank you for being so loving and supportive my entire life; I want you both to know how much I love you. To my sister, you have always been my rock, and I love you.

I also want to thank the woman in my life, Lori Leith, who has saved me in many ways. Lori, I am grateful for your love and support. Finally, I want to thank Justin Wargo and Daniel Collazo for becoming my brothers. It is when there is total collapse that you discover your true friends. Family doesn't end with blood.

Finally, I want to thank all of you for caring enough to read my rambles.

About the Author

Michael James Lutterschmidt is a forty-year-old Targeted Individual (TI) and author who is dedicated to exposing evil and corruption so that other people will be spared the pain and suffering he endures. His first book, *Extrajudicial Execution*, is an alarming memoir about his painful experience over a number of years.

www.ingramcontent.com/pod-product-compliance
Lightning Source LLC
Chambersburg PA
CBHW031508270326
41930CB00006B/315